GEOGRAPHY

FOR ~~CCEA GCSE~~ *wankers*

Revision Book

JENNIFER PROUDFOOT and GILLIAN REA

HODDER EDUCATION
PART OF HACHETTE LIVRE UK

The Publishers would like to thank the following for permission to reproduce copyright material:

CCEA Geography Compendium 2006–2007. © CCEA 2006–2007. Reproduced with the permission of the Northern Ireland Council for the Curriculum, Examinations and Assessment.

© G. Alexander 2006, p.105 (top).

Nelson Thornes, p.108. Reproduced with the permission of Nelson Thornes Ltd from 'The New Wider World Course Companion for CCEA GCSE Geography' by Peter Richardson. ISBN 0-7847-9081-0, first published in 2004.

The Office of Public Sector Information (OPSI), p.75. Reproduced under the terms of the Click-Use Licence.

Ordnance Survey, p.66. Reproduced by permission of Ordnance Survey on behalf of HMSO. © Crown copyright 2008. All rights reserved. Ordnance Survey number 100036470.

Bellanet, p.58.

p.4 © Michael Shake/Fotolia. www.fotolia.com.

Every effort has been made to trace all copyright holders, but if any have been inadvertently overlooked the Publishers will be pleased to make the necessary arrangements at the first opportunity.

Although every effort has been made to ensure that website addresses are correct at time of going to press, Hodder Education cannot be held responsible for the content of any website mentioned in this book. It is sometimes possible to find a relocated web page by typing in the address of the home page for a website in the URL window of your browser.

Hachette's policy is to use papers that are natural, renewable and recyclable products and made from wood grown in sustainable forests. The logging and manufacturing processes are expected to conform to the environmental regulations of the country of origin.

Orders: please contact Bookpoint Ltd, 130 Milton Park, Abingdon, Oxon OX14 4SB. Telephone: (44) 01235 827720. Fax: (44) 01235 400454. Lines are open 9.00–5.00, Monday to Saturday, with a 24-hour message answering service. Visit our website at www.hoddereducation.co.uk

© Jennifer Proudfoot and Gillian Rea 2008

First published in 2008 by
Hodder Education,
An Hachette Livre UK Company,
338 Euston Road
London NW1 3BH

Impression number   5 4 3 2 1
Year   2013 2012 2011 2010 2009 2008

Cover image: River Bann flood by Tony Hendron
Illustrations by GreenGate Publishing Services and Alex Machin
Typeset in Frutiger by GreenGate Publishing Services, Tonbridge, Kent
Printed in Malta

A catalogue record for this title is available from the British Library

ISBN: 978 0340 946 374

CONTENTS

Chapter 1 Introduction   1

Chapter 2 Theme A: Atmosphere and Human Impact   7

    Unit 1   Weather patterns and forecasting   7

    Unit 2   Variations in climate lead to different
                      interactions with environments   14

    Unit 3   Impact of human activities upon the
                      atmosphere and the environment   19

    Knowledge tests   21

Chapter 3 Theme B: Physical Processes and Challenges ✓   23

    Unit 1   Crustal movements and the impact
                      on people and the environment   23

    Unit 2   Rivers and river management   29

    Unit 3   Limestone landscapes and their
                      management   41

    Knowledge tests   45

Chapter 4 Theme C: Ecosystems and Sustainability ✓   47

    Unit 1   Distinct ecosystems develop in response
                      to climate and soils   47

    Unit 2   Human interference and upsetting the
                      balance of ecosystems   52

    Unit 3   Management of ecosystems and
                      sustainable development   59

    Knowledge tests   61

Chapter 5 Theme D: Population and Resources ✓   **63**

      Unit 1   Distribution and density   63

      Unit 2   Population changes over time   67

      Unit 3   Population growth and sustainability   77

      Knowledge tests   82

Chapter 6 Theme E: Economic Change and Development ✓   **84**

      Unit 1   Economic change creates new opportunities   84

      Unit 2   The impact of global economic change   89

      Unit 3   Sustainable development strategies   92

      Knowledge tests   101

Chapter 7 Theme F: Settlements and Change ✓   **102**

      Unit 1   Settlement development   102

      Unit 2   Urban growth and change   106

      Unit 3   Planning sustainability for urban
                            environments   112

      Knowledge tests   116

Chapter 8 Answers to Knowledge Tests and Tasks   **118**

Glossary Terms   **130**

Chapter 1 INTRODUCTION

Why use this book?

Exam success always depends on two things:

1 your knowledge and understanding of the subject matter
2 your ability to use that knowledge in the manner that will gain most marks in the examination.

To help you to gain your best possible grade, this book aims

◆ to set out the subject content essential to the CCEA GCSE Geography course
◆ to give you hints and revision tips which help you to understand and memorise the material
◆ to advise you on the best way to approach various types of exam questions.

Each chapter covers one of the six themes making up the GCSE course, as well as providing tasks, knowledge tests and exam questions from past papers so that you can check, as you go along, how much you understand and can remember. The answers are set out in the final chapter. The Glossary provides clear and concise definitions of the key ideas required for each topic. This section is important as you will almost certainly be asked to define some of them in the examinations.

Structure of the examination

In addition to coursework (worth 20% of the overall marks), which is completed and assessed in school, there are two examination papers, each worth 40% of the total marks.

Paper 1	Paper 2
3 physical geography themes • Atmosphere and human impact • Physical processes and challenges • Ecosystems and sustainability	3 human geography themes • Population and resources • Economic change and development • Settlements and change
You must answer all 3 questions, one on each theme	You must answer all 3 questions, one on each theme
Each question is made up of several parts, including both short answers and extended writing	Each question is made up of several parts, including both short answers and extended writing
Time: 1.5 hours Spend 30 minutes on each question	Time: 1.5 hours Spend 30 minutes on each question

Further details of the specification, including the requirements for each of the six themes, can be downloaded from the CCEA website at www.ccea.org.uk.

Revision techniques

For a full discussion of study skills and how to achieve exam success, see *Geography for CCEA* GCSE by Kay Clarke, Lynda Francis, Petula Henderson and Cormac McKinney, for which this book is a companion volume.

Here are some important recommendations about revision:

◆ Ideally, revision should be ongoing throughout the two-year course. Don't leave it all to the days just before the exam.
◆ Case studies, in particular, should be memorised as you go along so that facts about each one are clear in your mind before you study the next.
◆ Revision is **not** just re-reading your notes or textbook.
◆ It should involve reworking the subject matter, perhaps into a spider diagram or by summarising into brief bullet points.
◆ Next you have to memorise the material by repeating it to yourself, explaining it to someone else, writing a list or making a poster.
◆ Test yourself, to see how much your memory has retained, by writing out the bullet points or list, re-drawing the diagram or explaining it all to someone – this time without the help of your notes or book.
◆ Visual forms of revision, such as spider diagrams and learning maps can be a big help. They let us picture the key points, arrange them under headings and see connections.
◆ Case studies need careful revision, with facts, figures and places committed to memory. Writing the title of each one with bullet points covering the main ideas (including the facts, figures and place names) on a card will help you to concentrate on this aspect of the course. Gradually you will build up a collection of cards, ready for last-minute revision on the eve of the exam.

Do	Rework	Memorise	Write an answer
Stage 1	*Stage 2*	*Stage 3*	*Stage 4*
• Do classwork. • Do homework. • Do make notes highlighting key words and relevant facts: places, figures and names.	• Change notes into spider diagrams or learning maps. • Add own ideas/ theory and make links with previous notes. • Discuss your work with the teacher or a friend. • Make a summary box and structure the information under meaningful headings. • Find new ways of thinking about something, e.g. using thinking skills.	• Commit to memory by repetition. • Say the information out loud or make up a rhyme or tune. • Explain your topic to a friend. • Put the information up on posters around your room and move around when learning. • Take small breaks. • Close your notes. • Recall information by writing it out.	• Select the information which is relevant to answer a GCSE question. • Compose an answer to the question.

Examination techniques

COMMAND WORDS

In order to answer exam questions correctly, it is important to be sure what the examiner is really asking. Read the question carefully and underline the command words – these are words such as state, describe or explain. They tell you what to do in your answer. If you explain when asked to describe you will earn no marks, even if what you write is otherwise correct.

The following table gives the meanings of some of the command words you will meet.

Command word	Meaning
State	A short answer, presenting a fact or facts (e.g. the temperature in January, taken from a graph)
Describe	A descriptive answer **without** trying to explain When describing a **graph**, it is important to **quote figures** When describing a **map**, it is important to mention **place names**
Explain	Give a reason or reasons
Describe and explain	Make descriptive statements **and** give the reasons why (e.g. describe the pattern of rainfall shown on a map and explain why it falls there)
Label	Add labels to a diagram
Complete	Add information to a graph or a table so that it is complete
Match	Match statements that have been presented in the form of 'heads and tails'
State fully	This is often used when a reason is required in as much detail as possible
State the meaning	Usually used for definitions. You need to show that you know what the term means
Suggest	This is used when there may be more than one correct answer and any relevant one is acceptable

DIFFERENT TYPES OF QUESTION

Recall questions

These are designed to test your knowledge. Definitions of key ideas are in this category, e.g. 'State the meaning of the term earthquake'.

Data response questions

These questions may be based on a table of data, graph, Ordnance Survey (OS) map, photograph, sketch map, weather map, cartoon or newspaper article. They test what you can observe from the map or diagram and what you understand from what you have seen. These questions can make it easier to gain marks than with recall questions, since they provide you with visual clues, so try to make the best use of them.

◆ Tables and graphs

If you are asked to describe a graph or table, you need to put into words what it shows, remembering to quote some figures to support your statements.

◆ OS maps

An OS map is included with every examination, either with paper 1 or 2. A key to the symbols is printed alongside the map and the scale will be 1:50,000. This means that 2 cm on the map represents 1 km on the ground, and every grid square is 1 km x 1 km. You need to be able to:

1   measure accurately the distance in kilometres between points on the map. (Remember to bring a ruler to the examination.)
2   find features on the map using 4-figure and 6-figure grid references.
3   use compass directions to say, for example, that farm A is north-east of village B. Use only the eight compass points – N, NE, E, SE, S, SW, W, NW.
4   read the height above sea level from contour lines, spot heights or triangulation pillars and interpret relief shown by contour patterns.
5   apply your knowledge and understanding of the various themes (e.g. settlement, economic activity, limestone scenery and rivers) to evidence presented in the OS map.

◆ Photographs

In an exam you may be asked to match up a photograph with a location on an OS map or to comment on the geographical feature shown in the picture. Try to make full use of the evidence presented in the photograph.

◆ Weather maps

Look at the pattern of the isobars. If the highest pressure is in the centre, it shows an anticyclone with descending air, calm conditions and clear skies. If the lowest value is in the centre it shows a depression with rising air, and cloud and rain along the fronts. Take note of the time of day and date stated alongside the map as these help to explain the situation presented. By looking at the wind direction you may be able to suggest what air mass is influencing the area. A key is provided for the symbols used on the map, e.g. cloud cover and wind speed.

Levels of response questions

These are questions worth 6 marks or more, and they require extended written answers. For a 6-mark question, the mark scheme may be:

Level 1	1–2 marks	a correct but simple answer
Level 2	3–4 marks	a fuller answer, developing the basic idea
Level 3	5–6 marks	an answer showing greater depth of understanding

Example of a 'levels of response' question include 'State fully why…' or 'State fully how…'. There are likely to be 3 marks for each full explanation. To earn these 3 marks you need to:

◆ make a statement
◆ give a reason or consequence of the statement
◆ elaborate on the reason or consequence. This can be further detail or an actual named example.

Here is how you might answer the question: 'Study the diagram showing the original site of Belfast. State fully two reasons why this site would have been attractive to settlers.' (6 marks)

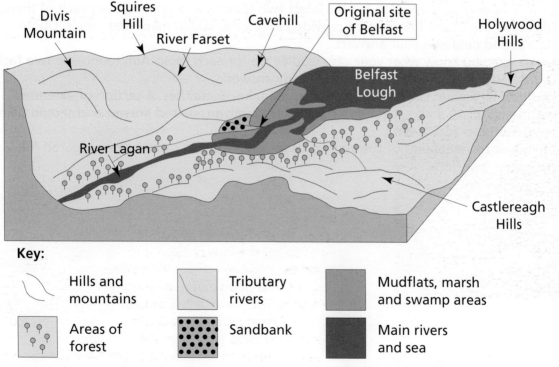

Key:

Hills and mountains	Tributary rivers	Mudflats, marsh and swamp areas
Areas of forest	Sandbank	Main rivers and sea

First reason	Second reason
• Statement: People can get wood from the woodland **(1)** • Consequence:…which they need to cook their food **(1)** • Elaboration:…or to build their houses **(1)**	**Either (for 2 marks):** It is near a river **(1)** which they could get water from to drink and cook with **(1)** **Or (for 3 marks):** The diagram shows it is near the Lagan and Farset Rivers **(2)** which they could get water from to drink or cook with **(1)**

Case studies

Case study questions are levels of response questions in which you need to show that you are writing about a real place. The facts should be as specific as possible, for example mentioning countries by name rather than referring to LEDCs or 'Africa'. For top marks you should aim to include at least **two facts** (figures, names or places) that are specific to the place you are writing about. For example, when writing about the Yorkgate Change in Function case study, 'creating 350 tertiary jobs' is worth more marks than 'creates new jobs' and 'Gallaher's tobacco factory' is better than 'a disused factory'.

Seven secrets of success

1 Answer all the questions. If you come to a question you think you can't do, think again but then leave it and go on to the next. When you have finished what you can do first time round, go back to the beginning and attempt any questions not answered. Do not sit doing nothing, but use all of the time available.

2 Read each question carefully. Underline command words in the question (e.g. <u>describe</u>, <u>explain</u>, <u>two examples</u>) to help you focus on keeping your answer relevant.

3 Follow instructions. When asked, for example, for two reasons do not give a list of three or four as only two will earn marks. Select two reasons and elaborate on each of them.

4 Make full use of the information provided in graphs, sketch maps and tables. Quote figures and details in your answers.

5 Make sure you know what your case studies are for each topic. Aim to include **two facts** (figures, names or places) in each case study answer.

6 Watch your timing. Each full question should take 30 minutes. A section of extended writing worth 10 marks requires a detailed, logically presented answer and should take ten minutes of your time.

7 Memorise the meanings of the key words for each topic in order to be prepared for definition questions.

Chapter 2 THEME A: ATMOSPHERE AND HUMAN IMPACT

Unit 1 – Weather patterns and forecasting

Elements of weather, units of measurement and instruments

You need to:
- *be able to name the instruments and units used to measure the five elements of weather shown in Figure 2.1.*
- *be able to give temperature or pressure readings from a photograph or drawing of an instrument.*

Weather is the day-to-day condition of the **atmosphere**. It includes the **elements of weather** shown in Figure 2.1.

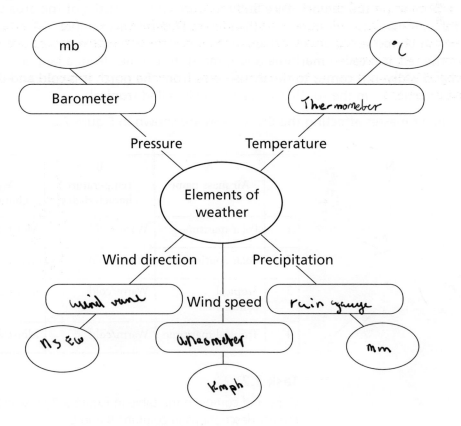

Figure 2.1

Task 2.1

Copy and complete Figure 2.1 by selecting an instrument and appropriate units from the two following lists. The first one is done for you.

Instruments	Units
rain gauge	°C
barometer	millimetres (mm)
wind vane	Knots per hour (kph)
maximum/minimum thermometer	millibars (mb)
anemometer	eight points of the compass (N, NE, E, SE, S, SW, W, NW)

Air masses

You need to:
- *know the names as well as the temperature and moisture characteristics of the four main air masses that affect the British Isles.*

An **air mass** is a large body of air (think of a giant 'blob' of air, perhaps the size of Western Europe) which takes on the temperature and moisture characteristics of the area where it is situated. If the air mass is stationary over the Sahara Desert, for example, then it becomes hot and dry. It then moves, as an air stream, and brings those characteristics with it. If it comes from the sea, it is called **maritime** and is moist. If it comes from a land area it is called **continental** and is dry. If it comes to the British Isles from the north it is cold and is called **polar**, but if it comes from the south it is warm and is called **tropical**.

The four main air masses affecting the British Isles are shown in Figure 2.2.

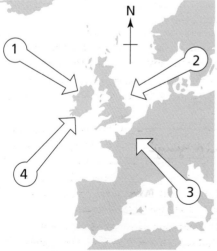

	A Air mass name	B Temperature characteristics	C Moisture characteristics
1	Polar maritime	Warm/cold	Moist/dry
2	Polar continental	Warm/cold	Moist/dry
3	Tropical continental	Warm/cold	Moist/dry
4	Tropical maritime	Warm/cold	Moist/dry

Figure 2.2

Task 2.2

Copy and complete the table in Figure 2.2 by selecting the correct descriptions in columns B and C.

Reasons for variability in weather patterns

You need to:

- *know what weather occurs in different parts of a depression – at the warm and cold fronts and in the warm sector*
- *know the sequence of change in the weather as a depression moves over a location*
- *know what the weather is like during winter and summer anticyclones*
- *know how rainfall is affected by relief.*

ANTICYCLONES AND DEPRESSIONS

Anticyclones and **depressions** are weather systems which determine the weather of the British Isles and allow us to make weather forecasts.

Comparison of anticyclones and depressions

	Anticyclone	Depression
Definition	An area of **high pressure**	An area of **low pressure** (*Easy to remember – if you're depressed, you're feeling 'low'*)
Air movement	Air is **sinking**	Air is **rising**
Cloud cover	**Clouds cannot form**	As it rises, air cools and condenses to form clouds
Wind speed	Winds are **gentle**, blowing **out** from the centre of high pressure. The isobars are far apart	Winds are **strong**, blowing **into** the centre of low pressure. The isobars are close together
Wind direction	Winds generally blow **clockwise** (*Remember – **anti**cyclone and **anti**clockwise do not belong together*)	Winds generally blow **anticlockwise**
Duration	Anticyclones are slow-moving so weather **remains the same** for several days or even a week or more	A depression moves quickly so the whole depression can pass over a particular location in around **24 hours**
Weather	<ul><li>Always **dry**; **little or no cloud**; **calm or gentle wind**</li><li>In **summer**, day temperatures are **high** (because of cloudless skies), night temperature can be **cool** as the earth's heat radiates into the atmosphere</li><li>In **winter**, day temperature is **low** because days are short and sun is not powerful. At night **cloudless skies** allow the temperature to fall below 0 °C and **frost** forms. Air near the ground is chilled and any moisture in it condenses to form **fog**</li></ul>	A **predictable sequence of weather** occurs as the depression moves over any location 1 First the warm front approaches. At the front warm air rises over cold air so clouds form and rain falls 2 Between the fronts is the warm sector, so temperatures rise a little, heavy rain stops and there may be some drizzle 3 The cold front arrives. Again the warm moist air is lifted over the cold air so clouds and heavy rain occur 4 Following the fronts, there is the cold sector, with lower temperatures. Cloud breaks up and showers become fewer

Task 2.3

1 In the table on page 9, each row of information follows logically from the row above. Make sure that you can follow the logic and then draw out a simpler version of the table to show the key points, which are printed in **bold**. Remember that, in almost every way, the characteristics of a depression and an anticyclone are the **opposite** of each other.

2 The table below presents a list of ways in which anticyclones and depressions can have an impact on people. Copy the table and complete the final column by writing D beside the statements that are true for depressions, SA for summer anticyclones and WA for winter anticyclones.

Human impact	D, SA or WA
1 Trees blown down, blocking roads	D
2 Drought creates problems for farmers and gardeners	SA
3 Sequence of rain, showers and bright intervals ensure that crops have sufficient moisture	D
4 Fog affects road-users and causes delays for aircraft	WA / DWA
5 Heavy rain may cause flooding	D
6 Icy, slippery footpaths cause increased injuries to elderly pedestrians	WA
7 TV weather forecasts advise the use of raincoats and umbrellas	D
8 Lots of sunshine ripens crops	SA
9 Increased sales of ice cream and suntan lotion	SA

Relief rainfall

When moist air rises, it cools and condenses to form clouds and then rain falls. In the case of **relief rainfall** it is a range of hills or mountains (known as relief) that causes the moist air to rise.

Task 2.4

Using the key provided, match the letters A–F to Figure 2.3 to provide appropriate labels at points 1–6.

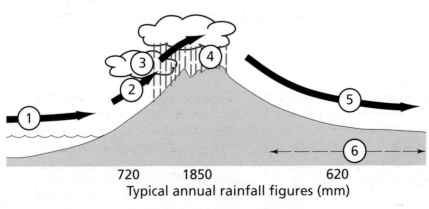

720   1850   620
Typical annual rainfall figures (mm)

A descending air gets warmer and drier
B warm moist air over ocean
C most rain falls
D condensation occurs – clouds form
E air rises and cools when it reaches mountains
F less rain falls in rain shadow area

Figure 2.3

Forecasting

You need to:
- *be able to interpret both satellite images and synoptic charts, distinguishing between depressions and anticyclones. A key is always provided with a synoptic chart so symbols do not need to be memorised*
- *be able to predict what weather is likely to occur next*
- *know that forecasts can be made for the short, medium and long term*
- *know of people who make use of weather forecasts.*

A **weather forecast** is a prediction of the weather expected in an area. It may be for the next 24 hours (short term), the next five days (medium term) or the next month (long term). A long-term forecast is less precise and dependable than the forecast for the next 24 hours.

Users of forecasts include:

◆ farmers and builders, who want to know if the weather will allow them to proceed with outdoor work
◆ supermarket managers who want to know whether to stock up with barbeque food and ice cream in a heat wave or with pies and soups for a chilly spell.

Task 2.5

'Having an accurate weather forecast could help to save the lives of motorists and sailors.'

Give **two** reasons for each group of people to explain why this statement is true.

SATELLITE IMAGES

These are photographs taken from space and sent back to earth. On a satellite image a depression will show up as swirls of white cloud along the fronts, on a dark background. An anticyclone will be shown as clear skies, allowing the land and its coastline to be visible.

SYNOPTIC CHARTS

Synoptic charts are weather maps that summarise the weather at a particular time. The date and time of day are clearly stated and should be noted as they help with the interpretation. A depression will have **fronts** (which are the boundaries between air masses) known as warm, cold and possibly occluded (see Figure 2.4) and the isobars are close together with the **lowest** value in the centre. Anticyclones have isobars that are further apart and the **highest** value is in the centre.

Symbols on a synoptic chart		
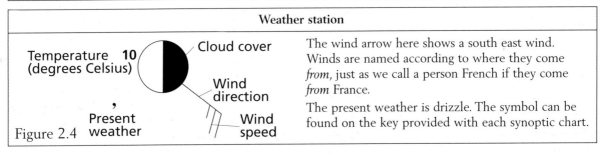		
Warm front	Cold front	Occluded front
Semi-circles like drawings of the sun reminding you of warmth. Always moves from west towards east	Shapes like jagged teeth reminding you of a cold 'biting' wind. Always moves from west towards east	This symbol is a mixture of both shapes. Found where warm and cold fronts meet

Weather station

Temperature **10** (degrees Celsius)

Cloud cover

Wind direction

Wind speed

Present weather

Figure 2.4

The wind arrow here shows a south east wind. Winds are named according to where they come *from*, just as we call a person French if they come *from* France.

The present weather is drizzle. The symbol can be found on the key provided with each synoptic chart.

2006 Past Paper Exam Questions

1   (b) Study Figures 2a and 2b which show the weather systems over the British Isles on 15 and 16 September 2004.

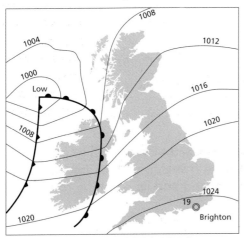

Figure 2a Sept 15, 2004 12 Noon

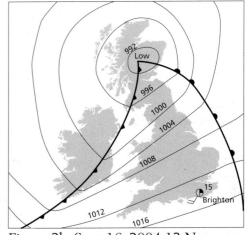

Figure 2b Sept 16, 2004 12 Noon

Key:

Cloud cover
oktas

○ 0	◑ 5		
◐ 1	◕ 6		
◖ 2	◗ 7		
◔ 3	● 8		
◑ 4	⊗ Sky obscured, e.g. by fog		

Wind direction

Northerly
Easterly

Fronts

▬●▬●▬ Warm
▲▬▲▬▲ Cold

Wind speed

◎ Calm
1–2 knots
3–7 knots
8–12 knots
13–17 knots
18–22 knots

Weather conditions

● Rain
◗ Drizzle
═ Mist
≡ Fog
↖ Thunderstorm

There is a key for you to refer to here, so read it carefully. The answer is 'warm front'.

To get 2 marks you have to give enough detail. For example, 'front moved east across Britain to North Sea'.

This question follows the statement, consequence, elaboration pattern we discussed in chapter 1. Statement – there was no cloud – 1. Statement and consequence – there was high pressure so no cloud formed so there was sunshine – 2. Statement, consequence and elaboration – air was sinking, giving high pressure, so no cloud formed, so there was sunshine and temperatures went up – 3.

1024 – take the nearest option. Look carefully at the correct diagram!

Answer the questions which follow.

Higher

(i) State the value of pressure over the south coast of England on 15 September (Figure 2a). (1)

(ii) 1 Name the front over Ireland on 15 September (Figure 2a). (1)
2 Describe how the location of this front changed from 15 September (Figure 2a) to 16 September (Figure 2b). (2)

(iii) The weather at Brighton on 15 September (Figure 2a) was warm and sunny. Explain why this was so. (3)

(iv) By 16 September (Figure 2b) the weather at Brighton had changed. Select **two** elements of the weather and explain why each changed. (6)

Foundation

(i) Underline the pressure value shown for the area near Brighton on 15 September (Figure 2a).
1016 mb   1020 mb   1024 mb   (1)

(iii) Describe the weather at Brighton on 15 September (Figure 2a) by underlining the statement which completes each sentence below correctly.
1 Brighton is **in the warm sector/ahead of the warm front**.
2 It is **cold and wet/warm and dry** in Brighton.
3 **There is no wind/It is windy** at Brighton. (3)

Be careful with this – the isobar is not right on the South Coast. Check for the direction the numbers go in – they are increasing towards the south, so it must be more than the closest isobar. The answer is 'Over 1024 mb' or 1024, 1025, 1026 or 1027 mb.

The clear skies on 15 September become cloudy by 16 September because Brighton is affected by a depression where air rises, cools and condenses to produce cloud.

There is no wind – again, the key gives you the meaning of the two circles inside each other.

It is warm and dry in Brighton – look at the synoptic symbol carefully and use the key.

Look carefully at the correct diagram! Brighton is ahead of the warm front.

Unit 2 – Variations in climate lead to different interactions with environments

Causes of variation in climate

You need to:
- *be able to define climate and four main climatic factors*
- *know how they affect the climate of Europe.*

Climate is the average weather taken over about 35 years. The four main climatic factors are:

- **Altitude** – height above sea level
- **Latitude** – distance from the equator
- **Continentality** – distance from the sea
- **Prevailing wind** – the most common direction the wind blows from.

Factor	Influence on climate
Altitude	• Temperatures fall by 1° C for every 100 metres of height • Rainfall is greater at high altitudes than in lowlands
Latitude	• The sun's rays are concentrated at the equator so places near the equator (low latitudes) are hotter than places near the poles where the sun's rays are spread out over a larger area and have less heating effect
Continentality	• Places near the sea are cooler in summer and warmer in winter than places inland • Places inland are drier than coastal areas because the winds blowing from the sea drop their rain at or near the coast
Prevailing wind	• Winds reaching Europe from the west cross the Atlantic Ocean and bring rain. They are cool in summer and mild in winter • Winds from the south bring warm dry weather to Europe from North Africa • Winds from the east in winter bring cold dry weather to Europe

Task 2.6

Copy and complete the table below. For each statement, tick one or more climatic factors and explain their effect. The first one is done for you.

Figure 2.5

Statement	Altitude	Latitude	Continentality	Prevailing winds	Explanation
1. The Alps often have snow all year	✓				They are mountains – it gets 1° C colder every 100 m up.
2. Rome is much hotter than Stensele		✓			closer to the equator
3. Ireland has much more rain than Moscow	✓			✓	rain full is greater at highend
4. Ireland has warmer winters and colder summers than Moscow			✓		

Impact of climate on farming

> **You need to:**
> - know how climate affects farming in two case studies – two different farms in different climates.

We have summarised what you need to know for the case studies used in *Geography for CCEA GCSE*. Your teacher may have given you different case studies – you can make a table like this and include the relevant information from your case studies.

	Farm in East Anglia between Norwich and Cambridge	Farm in Orgiva, southern Spain
Average temperature	• Summers warm, over 15 °C • Winters cold, 4 °C, frosts	• Summers hot, 25 °C • Winters mild, 10 °C
Rainfall	• Low rainfall – 650 mm all year	• Low rainfall – 450 mm all year. In summer this may go down to 5 mm in a month
Type of farming	• Arable – growing crops such as wheat, barley and potatoes	• Traditional farms on hills grow olives and grapes and keep sheep and goats • Now modern irrigation means they also grow oranges, lemons, peaches and vegetables
Positive influence on farming	• Low rainfall suits crop growing • Warm summers help crops ripen quickly, with 6.5 hours of sun per day in July • Cold winters and frost help break up soil and kill pests • August and September are quite dry so they can harvest crops easily	• Hot sunny summers help fruit ripen • Short cold winters help grapevines grow stronger, and kill pests • Mild winters suit orange and lemon trees • Rain in winter and spring helps olive trees produce olives
Negative influence on farming	• Sometimes it is too dry in the summer so crops do not grow successfully • If the frosts happen in spring they may kill young plants.	• Drought in summer means crops cannot grow • If there is frost in May it damages the vines • If there is too much rain, olive oil is too acidic to use, and wine from the grapevines is too watery
Role of technology in moderating impact of climate	• The farmers spray the crops with water (irrigation) • Some crops are protected from frost by heaters or polythene covers	• Rainwater from winter is stored and used to water crops in dry summers (irrigation). This means citrus fruit can grow as well as rice and cotton • Polythene tunnels make hothouses so vegetables can be grown all year.

Task 2.7

Copy and complete these spider diagrams to get the really important points clear in your head. Include a place name and two statistics. If you have different case studies, fill in the details for them instead.

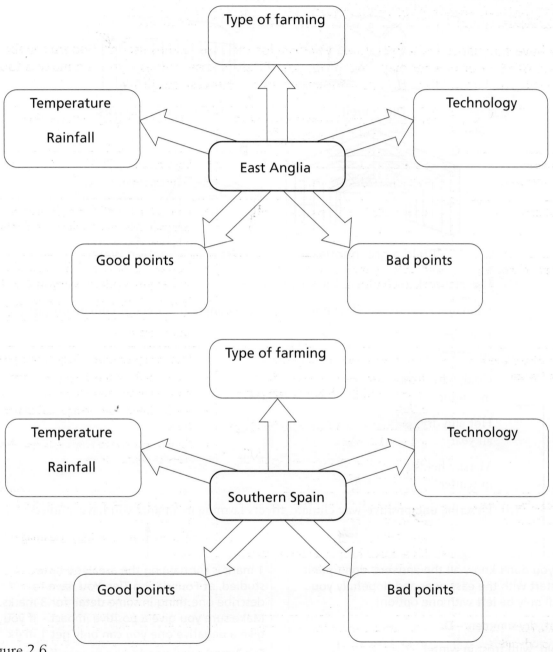

Figure 2.6

2006 Past Paper Exam Questions (Foundation Tier)

1 **(d)** Study Figure 4 which shows some ways technology is used to change the effect of climate on farming. Answer the questions which follow.

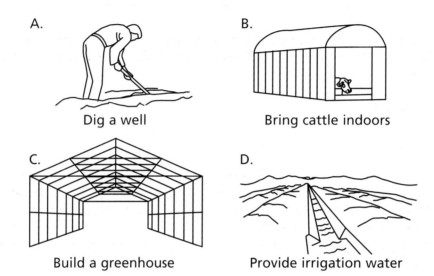

A. Dig a well

B. Bring cattle indoors

C. Build a greenhouse

D. Provide irrigation water

(i) Use Figure 4 to complete the spaces below. One has been completed for you.

Climate	Technology used to change the effect of climate on farming
Hot, dry summers	D
Cold, with frost in winter	B
Hot and dry all year	A
Marshy fields in winter	C

(3)

(ii) Describe **one** positive way climate affects farming in an area you have studied. (4)

If you don't know all the answers, don't panic – start with the easy ones and hopefully you will only be left with one option!

Hot, dry summers – D

Cold, with frost in winter – C

Marshy fields in winter – B

1 mark is for naming the area you have studied, at Foundation Tier. You have to describe one thing in some detail for 3 marks. Make sure you give a positive impact – if you give a negative one you can only get 1 mark

For 3 marks you need to be as specific as possible – 'In East Anglia warm summers over 15 °C help crops such as wheat and barley to ripen quickly.'

Unit 3 – Impact of human activities upon the atmosphere and the environment

Global warming – a global scale case study

You need to:
- *know some of the causes and impacts of global warming together with solutions and the need for international co-operation so that solutions are sustainable.*
- *remember at least two place names and two figures.*

This case study is summarised in a spider diagram on page 216 of *Geography for CCEA GCSE*, making it easier for you to memorise.

The greenhouse effect happens naturally and is not a problem in itself. The greenhouse gases in the atmosphere allow the sun's energy to reach and heat the earth but prevent much of this heat escaping back into space. The problem of **global warming** is due to the greenhouse effect being intensified, as more and more man-made greenhouse gases are added to the naturally occurring ones. Two of the most important greenhouse gases are **carbon dioxide** and **nitrogen oxides**.

Causes	Impacts (positive and negative)	Solutions
Carbon dioxide is increasing because of: • **burning fossil fuels** (coal, gas, oil) in vehicles and power stations • **deforestation** which reduces the number of trees taking CO_2 from the atmosphere and storing it as carbon Both of these increase as world population increases, along with standard of living and demand for energy **Nitrogen oxides** are produced by car engines. As car ownership increases in **MEDCs** and **LEDCs** this pollution increases too	**Sea level** is predicted to rise by up to 5 metres as a result of ice caps melting and also the expansion of seawater as it warms. Countries such as the Netherlands and Bangladesh, with low-lying coasts and high population density, are most at risk. Defensive sea walls will be very expensive **Climate change** will occur as more energy is trapped in the earth's atmosphere. Storms and hurricanes are likely to become more frequent, e.g. in southeast USA and the Caribbean. World rainfall patterns are likely to change with some places becoming wetter and others drier and this could lead to some endangered species of plants and animals becoming extinct **Tourism** could be affected with ski resorts in the Alps suffering from lack of snow and resorts such as Brighton in southern England attracting more visitors as sunshine increases. Positive outcomes for farming include production of vines and sunflowers in southern England.	**Reduce production of greenhouse gases:** • increase petrol prices so that people choose more fuel-efficient cars or use public transport • increase taxes on air travel so that people make fewer flights • build fewer coal, gas and oil-fired power stations and produce more renewable energy (solar, wave and wind power) **Afforestation:** Plant more trees so that more CO_2 is taken from the atmosphere and stored in plant material **International co-operation** is required as no single country can tackle this problem on its own. This has been attempted at Kyoto, Japan in 1997 when many countries agreed to reduce their greenhouse gas emissions by 5.2%. Also the **World Summit for Sustainable Development (WSSD)** at Johannesburg in 2002 set the target of reducing greenhouse gas emissions to 1990 levels

Task 2.8

Try adding details to these two spider diagrams to get the important points clear in your mind and reinforce them in your memory. Include place names and figures.

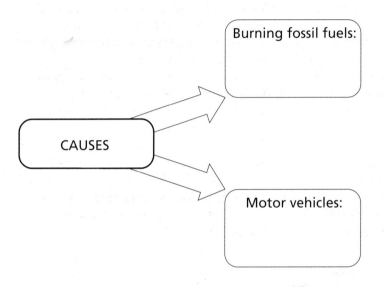

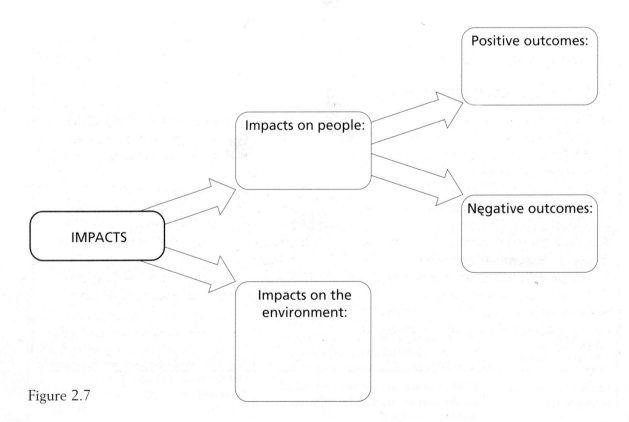

Figure 2.7

KNOWLEDGE TESTS

Knowledge Test I (Pages 7–13)

1 Name the instruments used to measure (a) windspeed (b) precipitation.
2 State the units of measurement of (a) pressure (b) temperature.
3 What is the name and characteristics of the air mass that influences the British Isles when winds are blowing from the north-west?
4 Does an anticyclone have (a) high or low pressure, and (b) air that is rising or sinking?
5 Where is rain to be expected in a depression: (a) the cold sector, (b) the warm and cold fronts, (c) the warm sector?
6 Which weather system, depression or anticyclone, brings strong winds?
7 Which weather system is responsible for fog and frost in winter?
8 What weather system, depression or anticyclone, is represented on a satellite image by a swirl of clouds on a dark background?
9 On a synoptic chart, what type of front has the symbol of a line of jagged 'teeth'?
10 Name two groups of people who find weather forecasts useful in their occupations.

KNOWLEDGE TESTS

Knowledge Test II (Pages 14–18)

1 True or false? (a) Temperature increases 1 °C for every 100 m increase in altitude. (b) Temperature decreases as distance from the equator increases.
2 When are coastal areas of Europe warmer than inland areas – summer or winter?
For the case study farm in East Anglia:
3 State the summer and winter temperatures and annual rainfall.
4 Name two crops produced.
5 Describe one way in which warm summers are a positive influence on farming.
6 Name one form of technology which can moderate the impact of climate.
For the case study farm in Orgiva, southern Spain:
7 State the summer and winter temperatures and annual rainfall.
8 Name two crops produced.
9 Describe one negative influence of climate.
10 Name one form of technology which can moderate the impact of climate.

KNOWLEDGE TESTS

Knowledge Test III (Pages 19–20)

1 What greenhouse gas is produced by deforestation and burning fossil fuels?
2 Why are nitrogen oxides increasing?
3 Why are people in the Netherlands and Bangladesh at severe risk from rising sea level?
4 How are southeast USA and the Caribbean at particular risk from climate change?
5 What two advantages could climate change bring for people in southern England?
6 What impact may climate change have on vulnerable plant and animal species?
7 Name three sources of renewable energy.
8 What term means to plant more trees?
9 How could increasing petrol prices help to reduce emissions of greenhouse gases?
10 What meeting in Johannesburg in 2002 set the target of reducing greenhouse gas emissions to 1990 levels?

Unit 1 – Crustal movements and the impact on people and the environment

Causes of plate movement

You need to:
- *know what plates are and how they are moved by convection currents in the mantle.*

The earth's structure can be divided into core, mantle and crust, as shown in Figure 3.1. The crust is not continuous and smooth, like the skin of an apple, but is made up of segments rather like the hexagons that make up a football. The segments of crust are known as **plates** and they are able to float on the semi-liquid mantle below. The intensely hot core heats the mantle and this causes **convection currents**. As these currents reach the top of the mantle and spread out, they drag the plates slowly apart (see plates B and C in Figure 3.1). When the convection currents cool and begin to sink back towards the core, they drag the plates above them closer together (see plates A and B in Figure 3.1).

Task 3.1

From the glossary, learn the definitions of:

a a plate
b convection currents.

Repeat them aloud to a pet, a parent or other member of your family.

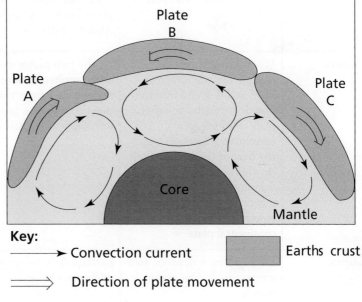

Figure 3.1 Convection currents in the mantle

Types of plate boundary

You need to:
- *be able to explain why earthquakes and/or volcanoes are found at constructive, destructive and conservative plate boundaries*
- *understand cross-section diagrams of each of these boundaries and be able to label features on them*
- *know the names of an example of each type of plate boundary.*

The edge of a plate, where it meets another, is called a plate boundary. A map of the world's plates showing destructive, constructive and conservative plate boundaries and the global pattern of earthquakes and **volcanoes** is found on page 31 of *Geography for CCEA GCSE*. The 'Ring of Fire' is the name of the zone of active volcanoes found along the edge of the Pacific plate.

What happens at different types of plate boundary?

	Destructive plate boundary	Constructive plate boundary	Conservative plate boundary
Plate movement	Plates come together	Plates move apart	Plates slide past each other
Explanation of name	Crust is destroyed	New crust is formed or constructed	Crust is conserved – neither destroyed nor added to
Examples	Boundary between South American plate and Nazca plate	Boundary between Eurasian plate and North American plate, known as the Mid-Atlantic ridge	The boundary between Pacific plate and North American plate – the San Andreas Fault
Processes	When plates meet, the oceanic plate is forced to bend and descend into the mantle beneath the other plate. This triggers earthquakes. Friction and the heat of the mantle melt the descending plate, forming magma. This magma rises and forms volcanoes on the continental plate	As the two plates move apart, molten rock or magma rises from the mantle to fill the gap, forming a new crust	Two plates slide past one another. Friction between them means that they tend to stick until pressure builds up and is released in a sudden-jerking movement, i.e. an earthquake
Features	Earthquakes, volcanoes, fold mountains and an ocean trench	Earthquakes, volcanoes and mid-ocean ridge	Earthquakes but no volcanoes

A: Destructive plate boundary
(cross-section)

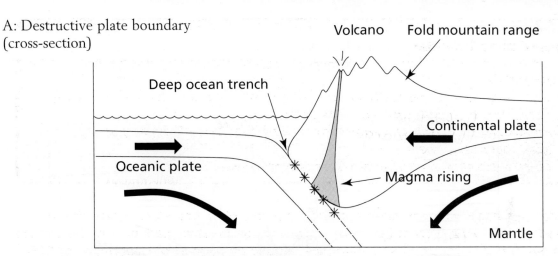

⁎ Earthquake focus (plural = foci,
so use foci if labelling a group
and focus for labelling one)

B: Constructive plate boundary
(cross-section)

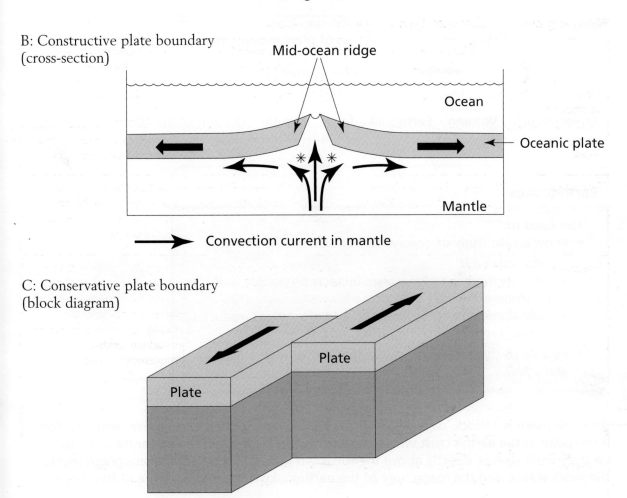

C: Conservative plate boundary
(block diagram)

Figure 3.2 Three types of plate boundary

Task 3.2

1 Copy and label this diagram of a plate boundary, choosing from the words in the box below it.
2 Show the direction of both convection currents by adding an arrowhead to each flow line.

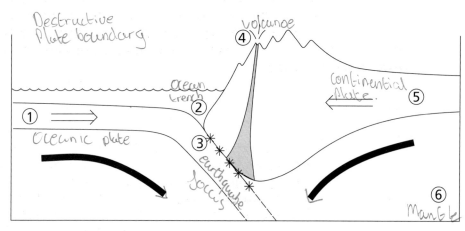

Figure 3.3

Key: ⟹ Direction of plate movement

▬▬▬ Convection current

Ocean trench	Volcano	Earthquake focus	Mantle	Oceanic plate	Continental plate

Earthquakes

You need to:
- *know a case study of one earthquake event, including:*
  - *what caused it*
  - *what its short- and long-term impacts on people and the environment were*
  - *how management, beforehand and afterwards, reduced, or could reduce, such negative impacts*
- *be able to contrast the management response in a LEDC and a MEDC.*

An **earthquake** is a shock, or series of shocks caused by a sudden earth movement. The **focus** is the point in the earth's crust where the earthquake occurs and the **epicentre** is the point on the earth's surface directly above the focus. An instrument called a **seismograph** records the shock waves, and the magnitude of the earthquake is measured on the **Richter** scale.

Case study of an earthquake event in a MEDC – Kobe, Japan

Date: 1995

Magnitude: 7.2 on the Richter scale

Causes: Japan is on a **destructive** plate boundary where two oceanic plates (the Pacific plate and the Philippine plate) are dipping underneath the Eurasian plate. The two oceanic plates experience friction as they bend and descend into the mantle, so pressure builds up. When the pressure is finally released it creates a severe earthquake.

Impacts

	Short term	Long term
Impacts on people	◆ 200,000 buildings collapsed ◆ 5,500 people died ◆ a 1 km stretch of the Hanshin Expressway collapsed ◆ 80% of quays in Kobe docks were destroyed ◆ more than 150 fires started by broken gas mains ◆ 1/4 million people made homeless, many camping outdoors in night temperatures of −2 °C	◆ water, gas and electricity not fully restored until six months later ◆ Hanshin Expressway closed for over a year ◆ homeless people living in temporary accommodation ◆ unemployment resulting from the closure of Mitsubishi and Panasonic factories
Impacts on the environment	◆ water in clay rock below parts of Kobe rose up making it liquefy into mud and causing collapse of buildings ◆ the ground moved 1.2 metres vertically and 2.1 metres horizontally	◆ most commercial buildings were repaired or replaced to higher safety standards

Management responses

Prediction and precaution before the event	Immediate and long-term strategies after the event
As earthquakes are common in Japan, precautions are taken: ◆ buildings are designed to withstand earthquakes, with springs or rubber pads to absorb the shockwaves ◆ earthquake drills every year, on the anniversary of the disastrous 1923 Tokyo quake, allow emergency teams and individuals to practise and improve their responses ◆ people keep earthquake kits (including blankets, bottled water, rice and a radio) in their homes	Immediate attempts by fire crews from Kobe and nearby Osaka and Kyoto to put out the fires Emergency shelter and food provided immediately from elsewhere in Japan In the longer term there have been: ◆ increased spending on research into earthquake prediction, e.g. by satellite detection of minute distortions in the earth's crust ◆ stricter building regulations such as flexible steel frames for high-rise buildings and fire-resistant materials for houses

Task 3.3

Try to draw your own spider diagram to sum up the Kobe earthquake, its causes, impacts and management responses. If you have a different earthquake case study, draw a diagram for it instead, making sure that you include all the headings from the Kobe study.

CONTRASTS IN RESPONSE BETWEEN A MEDC AND A LEDC

A MEDC, such as Japan, has greater economic wealth than a LEDC so it can afford to have:

◆ emergency teams that are better equipped and trained than in a LEDC
◆ buildings and bridges that are designed to withstand earthquakes. Money can be spent on researching building design and on enforcing building regulations
◆ road networks and communication systems that allow rescue teams and fire crews to reach the damaged areas quickly.

All these factors combine to minimise both deaths and damage when an earthquake occurs in a MEDC.

Name an earthquake you have studied. There is no mark for this but you do have to be specific to one earthquake to get top marks. This is a case study question, so you should be aiming to give details like place names and numbers.

2006 Past Paper Exam Questions (Higher Tier)

(e) Name an earthquake you have studied.
  1. Explain the cause of the earthquake. (3)
  2. State fully **two** strategies put in place after the event to reduce loss of life in future earthquakes. (6)

For 3 marks you need to give detail, including one fact or figure such as naming the plates. For example, 'Japan is on a destructive plate boundary where two oceanic plates (the Pacific plate and the Philippine plate) are dipping underneath the Eurasian plate. The two oceanic plates experience friction as they bend, so pressure builds up. When the pressure is finally released it creates a severe earthquake.'

State fully means you have to give some detail in your answer. The marks break down into 3 for each strategy – each one needs statement (S), consequence (C) and elaboration (E).
For example, 'they introduced stricter building regulations (S) so that buildings would be less likely to collapse and kill people (C). For example, high-rise buildings had to have flexible steel frames (E).
They increased spending on research into earthquake prediction (S), hoping to be able to give people warning to leave their homes if an earthquake was about to happen, so that they would be less likely to be killed (C). For example, they used satellites to detect tiny changes in the shape of the earth (E).'

Unit 2 – Rivers and river management

Characteristics of a drainage basin

You need to:
- *know about the features of a drainage basin*
- *be able to explain what changes in a river downstream and why*
- *understand erosion, transportation and deposition*
- *understand how meanders and floodplains are formed.*

Rivers are an important part of the **hydrological cycle**, or water cycle. This is the way water is evaporated from the sea, goes through the air and flows back to the sea through rivers or the ground.

FEATURES OF A DRAINAGE BASIN

Task 3.4

Match the letters A–E on Figure 3.4 to the following labels. One letter has two labels.

Drainage basin – the area of land drained by a river and its tributaries
Source – where a river starts
Tributary – stream flowing into river
Mouth – where a river flows into the sea
Watershed – highest point all around the drainage basin
Estuary – an area at the mouth of some rivers, wide and shallow, where the tide flows in and out

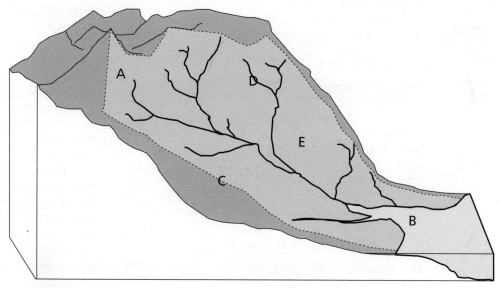

Figure 3.4

RIVER CHANNEL CHANGES DOWNSTREAM

Downstream means the way the river flows – from the source to the mouth.

Characteristic	Width	Depth	Discharge	Load
Meaning	Distance from one side of the river to the other	Measure from top of water to river bed. Take average across river	Amount of water passing a point in a certain time – cumecs (cubic metres of water per second)	The material a river is carrying – mud, sand, pebbles, rocks
Change that occurs as you go downstream	Gets wider	Gets deeper	Increases	Particles get smaller and more rounded
Reason for the change	The river erodes sideways as it travels (lateral erosion)	The river erodes downwards as it travels (vertical erosion)	More water flows into the river from each tributary. Water flows faster with less friction	Particles knock against each other and break each other up. Sharp angular edges get knocked off

Task 3.5

Copy and complete the table in Figure 3.5 choosing from the words in the box underneath.

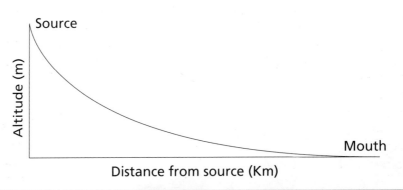

	Near source	Near mouth
Width		
Depth		
Discharge		
Load (2 words for each column)		

Figure 3.5

large   small   angular   rounded   narrow   shallow   deep   wide   high   low

FLUVIAL PROCESSES OF EROSION, TRANSPORTATION AND DEPOSITION

Fluvial processes are processes operating in rivers, such as erosion, transportation and deposition.

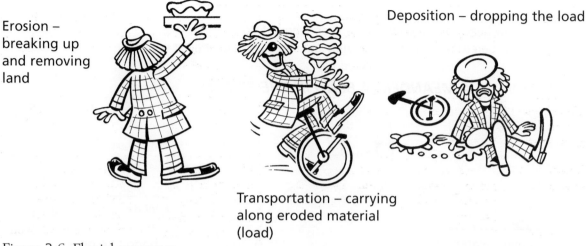

Erosion – breaking up and removing land

Transportation – carrying along eroded material (load)

Deposition – dropping the load

Figure 3.6 Fluvial processes

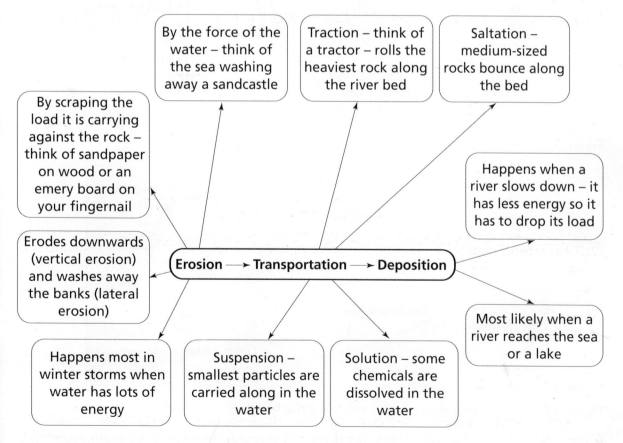

By the force of the water – think of the sea washing away a sandcastle

Traction – think of a tractor – rolls the heaviest rock along the river bed

Saltation – medium-sized rocks bounce along the bed

By scraping the load it is carrying against the rock – think of sandpaper on wood or an emery board on your fingernail

Happens when a river slows down – it has less energy so it has to drop its load

Erodes downwards (vertical erosion) and washes away the banks (lateral erosion)

Erosion → Transportation → Deposition

Most likely when a river reaches the sea or a lake

Happens most in winter storms when water has lots of energy

Suspension – smallest particles are carried along in the water

Solution – some chemicals are dissolved in the water

Figure 3.7

31

Task 3.6

For each of the following descriptions, decide what process is happening.

a Large pieces of rock are broken off the edge of the river bank.
b The river looks very brown because it is carrying lots of mud.
c During a flood the river got wider.
d There is a tiny beach at the edge of the river, where it flows into a lake.
e If you paddle barefoot in the river you may get stones hitting against your feet.

FORMATION OF A MEANDER (A BEND IN THE RIVER)

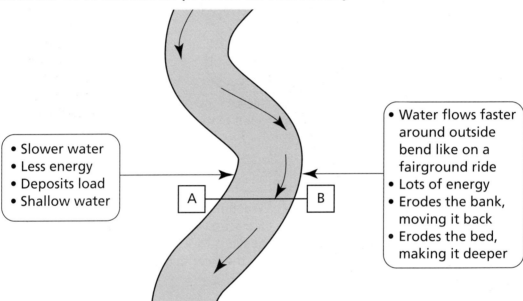

• Slower water
• Less energy
• Deposits load
• Shallow water

• Water flows faster around outside bend like on a fairground ride
• Lots of energy
• Erodes the bank, moving it back
• Erodes the bed, making it deeper

Figure 3.8 Formation of a meander

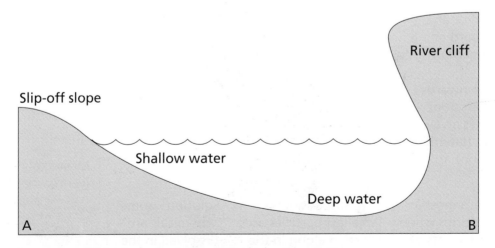

River cliff

Slip-off slope

Shallow water

Deep water

A

B

Figure 3.9 Cross-section through channel along the line A–B

Figure 3.9 shows what it would look like if you cut through the river. In an exam you might have to label these features on a diagram or a photo.

Task 3.7

1 Check you have understood the main facts about meanders. On your own copy of Figure 3.10:

◆ place the labels from the box on the right in the correct column on the diagram
◆ draw arrows to show where the water flows fastest in the river.

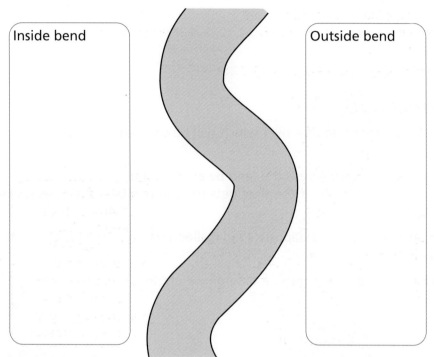

Inside bend

Outside bend

Faster flow
Slower flow
Lots of energy
Less energy
Erosion
Deposition
River cliff
Slip-off slope
Deep water
Shallow water

Figure 3.10

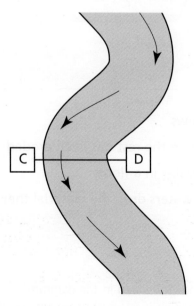

C   D

Figure 3.11

2 Draw a cross-section diagram of C–D from Figure 3.11.
Label:

- ◆ Fast-flowing water
- ◆ Slow-flowing water
- ◆ Deep water
- ◆ Shallow water
- ◆ Erosion
- ◆ Deposition
- ◆ River cliff
- ◆ Slip-off slope

FORMATION OF A FLOODPLAIN

A floodplain is the flat land either side of a river which will be covered in water if the river bursts its banks.

Where there are meanders, the river flattens the land by eroding it and depositing sediment on it, making a flat floodplain. If the river gets too full and bursts its banks, water floods over the floodplain.

The water slows down, loses energy, and deposits load (called sediment or alluvium) which is fertile (good for growing crops).

In an exam you might have to label (annotate) a diagram or photo.

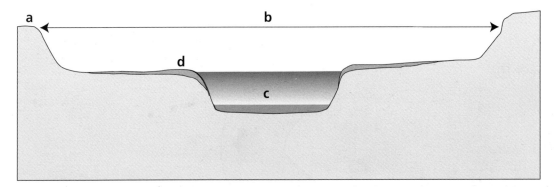

River channel – where the river flows

Bluff – remains of higher land, where the rest has been eroded

Floodplain – flat area covered in water in a flood

Deposition – process where flood waters drop the material they are carrying

Figure 3.12

Task 3.8

Match up the definitions above with the letters a–d in the diagram.

Flood hazard

You need to:
- *be able to explain what a flood is*
- *know what can cause a flood*
- *know what impacts a flood can have, what people try to do about it (the management response) and how we need a co-ordinated approach to ensure sustainable development.*

Flooding occurs when the water in a river is higher than the river bank, so it overflows.

Task 3.9

1 Copy and complete the flow diagrams below to summarise five causes of flooding. Use the phrases from the box below to fill in the gaps. Decide for each one whether it is a physical (natural) cause or a human cause (caused by people) and write P or H next to it. The first one has been done for you.

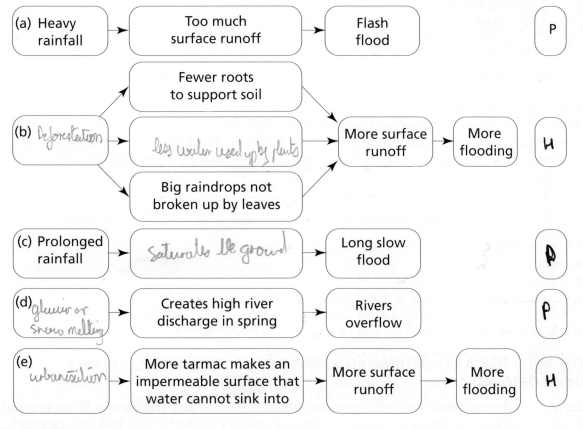

Figure 3.13

Deforestation   Less water used up by plants   Glacier or snow melting

Urbanisation   Saturates the ground

2 Copy and complete the table below to summarise the impacts of flooding. For each impact write + or – next to it to show if it is positive or negative. Colour each statement, either green, if it impacts the environment, or red, if it impacts people.

Impacts	Positive or negative
Fills up drinking water supplies	
Spreads disease	
People and animals can drown	
Provides water for crops	
Roads and railways may be disrupted	
Buildings can be damaged	
Provides sediment which makes soil more fertile for growing crops	
Crops growing on the floodplain may be washed away	
Land may get waterlogged so it cannot be farmed	
Provides a habitat for fish and shellfish which people can eat	
People may be made homeless	

MANAGEMENT RESPONSE

There are two main responses to flooding: hard engineering and soft engineering. Hard engineering involves building large structures to try to control the river. Soft engineering means trying to reduce flooding without damaging the river for future generations.

Task 3.10

Decide whether each of the following methods is an example of hard or soft engineering.

◆ Planting trees S
◆ Building dams h
◆ Building high embankments h
◆ Planting water-loving plants on the floodplain to soak up water S
◆ Making embankments set back from the river S
◆ Making the river channel deeper and wider h

THE NEED FOR A CO-ORDINATED APPROACH TO ENSURE SUSTAINABLE DEVELOPMENT

Sustainable development involves improving people's income and standard of living without using up resources, creating pollution or harming people's quality of life. This development must be sustainable – you must be able to keep it going for a long time without problems.

If people are going to live near rivers, they need to make sure that what they do to that river is sustainable. For example, if hard engineering causes problems further down the river, then it is not a sustainable type of development.

Different groups of people use rivers for:

◆ water supply for houses
◆ water supply for factories
◆ sports like boating and fishing
◆ transport.

Different groups of people use the floodplain for:

◆ building houses
◆ farming (**irrigation** – using water from the river to water the crops)
◆ factory building
◆ road building.

All these things happen all the way along the river. Anything that is done to the river in one place will affect what happens further downstream – for example, if too much water is removed, there will not be enough left further downstream. If too much water is channelled through the river too quickly in one area, it will reach another area too quickly and cause a flood.

All users of the river and its floodplain need to work together to make sure that any planned development avoids causing damage.

A river management scheme at the national/regional scale

You need to:
* *know one case study including:*
  * *causes of flooding*
  * *impacts of flooding*
  * *management response to flooding*
  * *why we need a co-ordinated approach so that sustainable development takes place*
  * *at least two place names and two statistics*
* *be able to write about all these things in general, as well as for your case study (at the higher tier).*

Case study of a river management scheme – the Mississippi

The Mississippi is the fourth longest river in the world. It is an essential river for the USA, providing 18 million people with their water supply. Flooding is an almost annual event.

Causes of flooding

Physical	Heavy rainfall in the Appalachian mountains
Human	◆ Urbanisation – lots of tarmac so water cannot soak into the soil. It flows quickly into the river ◆ Wetland areas (marshes) have been drained, so water is not stored but goes straight into the river ◆ Farming allows more surface runoff than natural grassland ◆ People have straightened the river so water flows down it more quickly ◆ People have built levees to keep the flood waters in. In 1993 these collapsed because of the weight of water

Impacts of flooding

	Positive	Negative
On people	Frequent flooding fertilises the soil Flat land is easy to build on Gentle slopes make the river good for transport	In 1993: ◆ $10.5 billion damage ◆ 45 people killed ◆ 74,000 people evacuated ◆ 9000 jobs lost in Illinois ◆ 45,000 houses destroyed
On the environment	Marsh areas got fresh water Lots of wildlife, e.g. beaver, bald eagle	Wildlife killed, lost food sources

Management response to flooding

Hard engineering	Soft engineering
Levees or embankments have been built (3000 km of them!) Engineers cut through the meanders to straighten the river 100 dams have been built to control the flow of the water	Tree planting (afforestation) in the Tennessee Valley – trees absorb water Diversion spillways for floodwater Safe flooding zones – houses near the river are bought and areas of floodplain are turned into green spaces Natural wetlands to be restored

Need for co-ordinated approach

Thirty-one states in the USA depend on the Mississippi. Engineers, conservationists and planners need to work together to enable building and economic activity to go ahead in a way that works with the river, and will not make the floods worse.

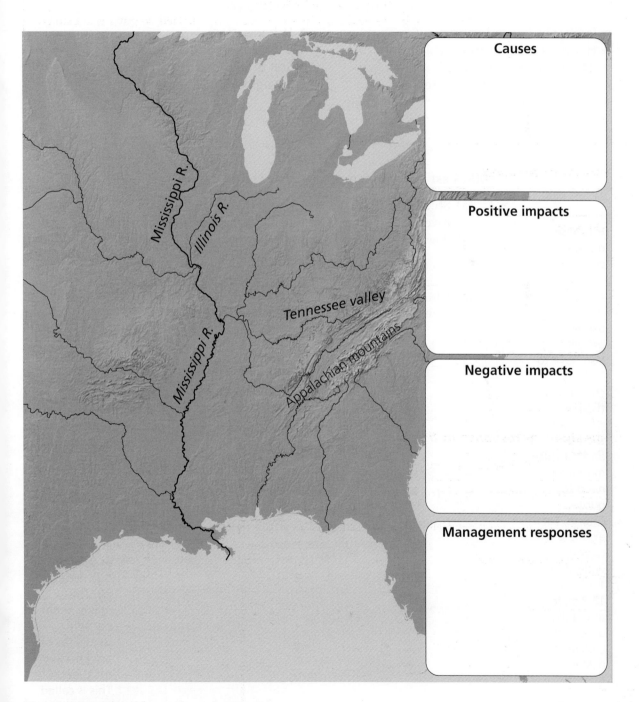

Figure 3.14 Flood hazard on the Mississippi

Task 3.11

Use the information from page 38 to add the following labels to a copy of the map (you could hand draw it – it doesn't have to be accurate, just include the important information). You will need to put some of them in the bubbles, and others can be written at specific places. You could simply put the labels under the correct heading without using a map, if you prefer.

- 9000 jobs lost in Illinois
- Heavy rainfall in Appalachians
- 74,000 people evacuated
- Marsh areas get fresh water
- Good habitat for beaver and bald eagle
- Urbanisation
- Wetland areas drained
- Soil is fertilised
- Straightening of river channel

2006 Past Paper Exam Questions (Higher Tier)

2 (a) Study Table 1 which shows how the Whitewater River in the Mourne Mountains changes downstream. Answer the questions which follow.

Table 1

Distance from source (km)	Width of river channel (m)	Depth of river channel (m)	Size of load. Longest axis (cm)
1	1.27	0.05	14
17	12.2	0.24	7

(i) Describe how the river channel changes downstream. (4)

(ii) The load is smallest near the mouth of the river. State fully **one** reason why this is so. (3)

This is a data response question – you can get marks very easily if you remember to use the data properly. You have to identify changes in the river channel (**not** the load) and for full marks you need to quote figures. For example 'The river gets wider from 1.27 m to 12.2 m. It also gets deeper from 0.05 m to 0.24 m'.

State fully one reason why this is so – make sure you give statement, consequence and elaboration. For example 'Rocks hit against each other and the river banks and river bed as they go downstream (S). This makes them become smaller as bits are knocked off them (C). This is called erosion (E).'

Unit 3 – Limestone landscapes and their management

Role of rock, structure and weathering process in creating the distinctive environment

You need to:
- *know about different types of rock, especially what limestone is like and how it is weathered away*
- *know how these things change the landscape.*

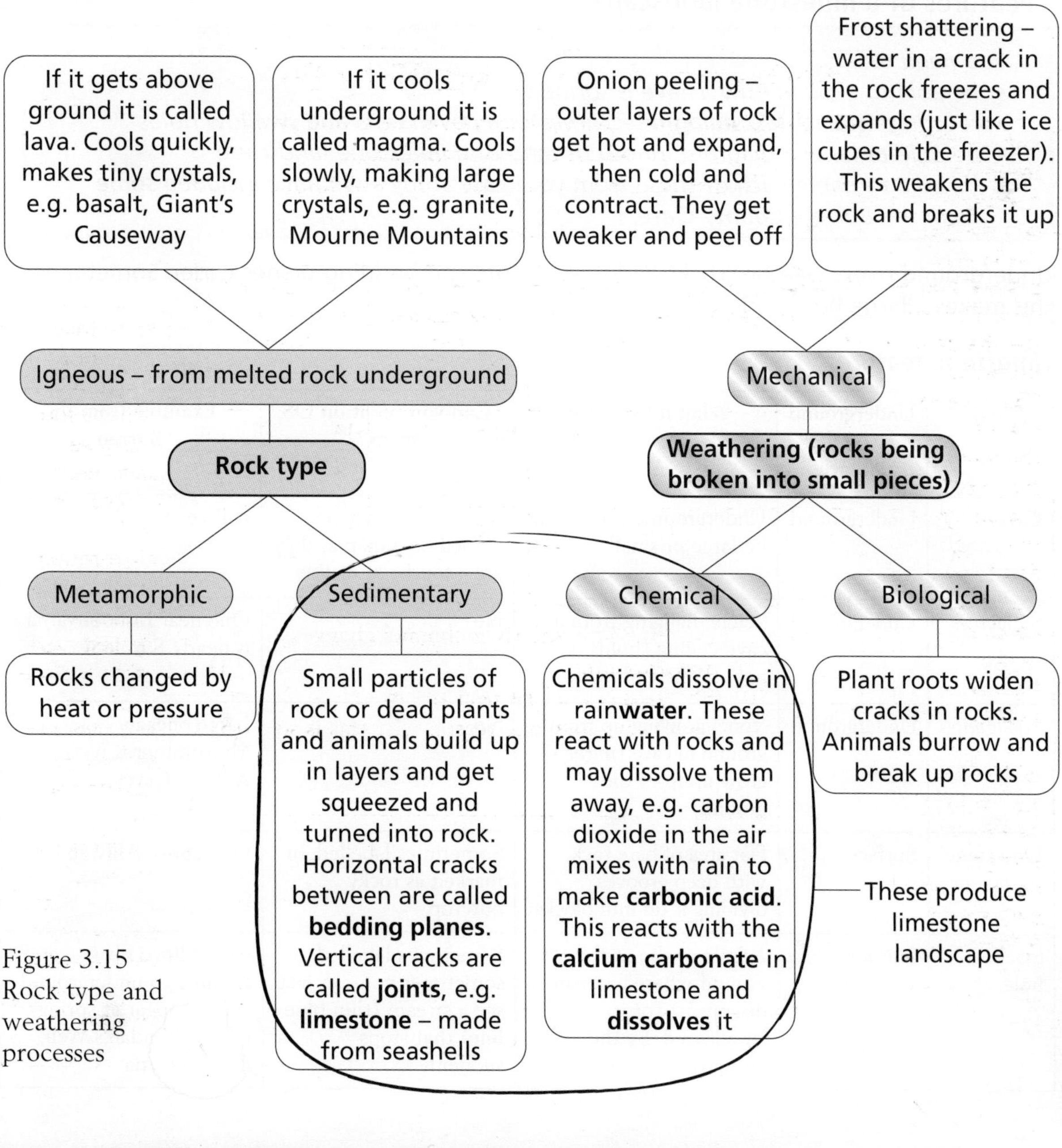

If it gets above ground it is called lava. Cools quickly, makes tiny crystals, e.g. basalt, Giant's Causeway

If it cools underground it is called magma. Cools slowly, making large crystals, e.g. granite, Mourne Mountains

Onion peeling – outer layers of rock get hot and expand, then cold and contract. They get weaker and peel off

Frost shattering – water in a crack in the rock freezes and expands (just like ice cubes in the freezer). This weakens the rock and breaks it up

Igneous – from melted rock underground

Mechanical

Rock type

Weathering (rocks being broken into small pieces)

Metamorphic

Sedimentary

Chemical

Biological

Rocks changed by heat or pressure

Small particles of rock or dead plants and animals build up in layers and get squeezed and turned into rock. Horizontal cracks between are called **bedding planes**. Vertical cracks are called **joints**, e.g. **limestone** – made from seashells

Chemicals dissolve in rain**water**. These react with rocks and may dissolve them away, e.g. carbon dioxide in the air mixes with rain to make **carbonic acid**. This reacts with the **calcium carbonate** in limestone and **dissolves** it

Plant roots widen cracks in rocks. Animals burrow and break up rocks

These produce limestone landscape

Figure 3.15
Rock type and weathering processes

Task 3.12

1 Copy and complete this paragraph, using the words in **bold** in Figure 3.15 to fill in the gaps.

_____ has a structure with lots of horizontal cracks called _____ and vertical cracks called _____. These allow _____ to flow through the rock.

_____ in the water reacts with the _____ in limestone and _____ it away. This makes lots of unusual landscape features (sometimes called karst landscape).

2 Copy Figure 3.15, cut it up and try to put the pieces together correctly – like a jigsaw.

Features of a limestone landscape

You need to:
- be able to explain how a cave is formed
- recognise stalactites, stalagmites, limestone pavements and swallow holes
- be able to label a diagram, photo or map of a limestone landscape
- be able to name each of these from your case study – we have included some from the Burren, County Clare.

Underground rivers weather rocks and make joints and bedding planes wider. Sometimes this makes a large hole underground, called a cave.

Limestone features

Feature	Underground or on the surface	What it looks like	Can you see it on OS maps?	Example from the Burren
Cave	Underground	Underground hole – can be large or small	Major caves may be named on a map as they are a tourist attraction	Aillwee Cave
Stala*ctites*	Underground	'icicle' hanging from a cave ceiling (holds on *tight* to the ceiling)	No	One near Lisdoonvarna is nearly 8 m long
Stala*gmites*	Underground	'cone' growing up from ground in cave (*might* grow up from the ground)	No	Large ones in Midsummer Cavern, Aillwee Caves
Limestone pavement	Surface	Flat area of bare rock, with deep grooves dividing it up into blocks	Sometimes labelled, or marked as rocky outcrop	One above Aillwee Cave
Swallow hole	Surface	A hole or dip in the ground where a stream disappears (or is 'swallowed' by the ground)	Sometimes labelled, or sometimes you can just see a stream (thin blue line) that stops suddenly	Near Slieve Elva – streams go underground and reappear at springs, e.g. St Brendan's Well, Lisdoonvarna

Task 3.13

1 Label the diagram with the features listed in the table.

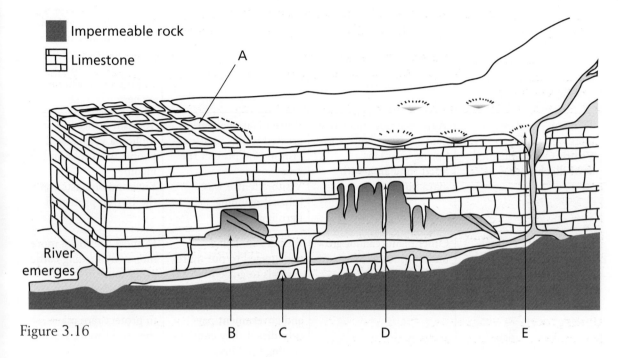

■ Impermeable rock

▥ Limestone

River emerges

Figure 3.16

2 If you are a visual learner, make a mental movie of what happens when a stream goes underground, remembering to include all the features in the table.

3 Copy the table, cut it up into squares and try to put each section back in the right order.

Human pressure in a limestone environment

You need to:
- *know how people use the limestone environment and why*
- *know what problems this use causes*
- *know what has been done about it*
- *know how different groups involved might disagree.*

Human pressure in the Burren, County Clare

Causes of pressure	Impact	Management response	Groups in conflict
Quarrying – flagstones have been cut in Moher area for years	Limestone is removed permanently Plants and animals lose habitat Noisy, unsightly	Banned by law	Local people want jobs Tourists dislike noise and think quarries are ugly. Environmentalists want to protect limestone scenery
Tourism – walkers, increased traffic Visitor Centre planned at Mullaghmore	Walkers erode limestone, damage rare plants, e.g. Spring Gentian Spoil rural area with extra buildings	Burren National Park created – tries to attract visitors and protect the area Visitor Centre was refused planning permission	Tourism brings in £56 million a year – local people want jobs and income Environmentalists want the Burren protected
Farming – not enough animals (undergrazing) so hazel shrubs can grow	Other plants cannot grow under shrubs. Biodiversity in some areas has decreased by 18%	Farmers are being encouraged to put more animals to graze the land – winter grazing season has been made longer, and government pays subsidies if they continue grazing the hills	Farmers can make more money by feeding cattle other food, in cattlesheds Environmentalists want to protect rare plants, so they want more grazing

Task 3.14

1 If you have a different case study, try putting the information from it into a table like the one above.
2 Turn your table into a spider diagram using the headings in the table above.

The answer is chemical.

Breaking up of rocks by the elements, e.g. rain, heat, cold.

This could be a cave, stalactite or stalagmite.

2006 Past Paper Exam Questions (Foundation Tier)

(ii) On the list below underline the main type of weathering which creates limestone pavements.

   Biological   Chemical   Physical   (1)

(iii) State the meaning of the term **weathering**.   (2)

(iv) Name **one underground** feature seen in limestone areas.   (1)

(v) For a named limestone area you have studied, state fully **one** way people may damage that area.

   Name of limestone area   (1)

   Damage   (3)

You get a mark for a named area at Foundation level, so try to think of one even if you can't remember much about it, e.g. the Burren. Then you need statement, consequence and elaboration, e.g. 'Tourists walking over the limestone might pick some of the flowers found in the Burren such as Mountain Aven. These are rare, so if they are all picked there will be no new seeds and they might die out.

KNOWLEDGE TESTS

Knowledge Test I (Pages 23–28)

1 What causes the plates of the earth's crust to move?
2 The Ring of Fire surrounds which ocean?
3 If plates move apart, is the plate boundary constructive or destructive?
4 At which type of plate boundary is an ocean trench formed?
5 Name an example of a conservative plate boundary.
6 What name is given to the point in the earth's crust where an earthquake occurs?
7 Name the plates involved in the 1995 Kobe earthquake in Japan.
8 How many people were (a) killed and (b) left homeless by the Kobe earthquake?
9 What caused the fires which were a major feature of the Kobe earthquake?
10 Suggest one reason why an earthquake in a MEDC would cause fewer deaths and less damage than a similar earthquake in a LEDC.

KNOWLEDGE TESTS

Knowledge Test II (Pages 29–40)

1 What is the term used for a stream flowing into a river?
2 What happens to large angular rocks and pebbles as a river carries them downstream?
3 What is meant by river discharge?
4 True or false? A river erodes on the outside bank of a meander bend because the water is deep and travelling fastest there.
5 True or false? A slip-off slope is found on the outside bank of a meander bend.
6 Where and why does deposition occur on a meander bend?
7 What is deposited on a floodplain as a result of flooding?
8 State one human cause of flooding.
9 Planting water-loving plants on a floodplain to soak up water is known as what type of engineering?
10 What positive impact does flooding in the Mississippi Basin have on the environment?

KNOWLEDGE TESTS

Knowledge Test III (Pages 41–44)

1 Is limestone a sedimentary, igneous or metamorphic rock?
2 What are the horizontal cracks in limestone called?
3 When rainwater containing carbonic acid acts on limestone, this is an example of what type of weathering?
4 Name two features found on the surface of a limestone landscape.
5 Does a stalagmite grow down from the ceiling or up from the floor of a limestone cave?
6 How much money does tourism contribute to the economy of the Burren area each year?
7 Name a rare plant that can be damaged by tourists walking in the Burren area.
8 What is the management response to quarrying which would permanently damage the Burren area?
9 By what percentage has biodiversity decreased in the Burren as a result of undergrazing (not enough animals)?
10 What is the management response to undergrazing?

Chapter 4 THEME C: ECOSYSTEMS AND SUSTAINABILITY

Unit 1 – Distinct ecosystems develop in response to climate and soils

Location and distribution of ecosystems

You need to:
- *know the main ecosystems round the world*
- *know how they are affected by climate and soil*
- *know about food webs*
- *know all this especially for one local ecosystem, and one tropical ecosystem.*

An **ecosystem** is a community of plants and animals and the environment in which they live. It includes the **soil**, air, water, rock and climate. A biome is a very large-scale ecosystem – a huge area with similar soils, plants and animals.

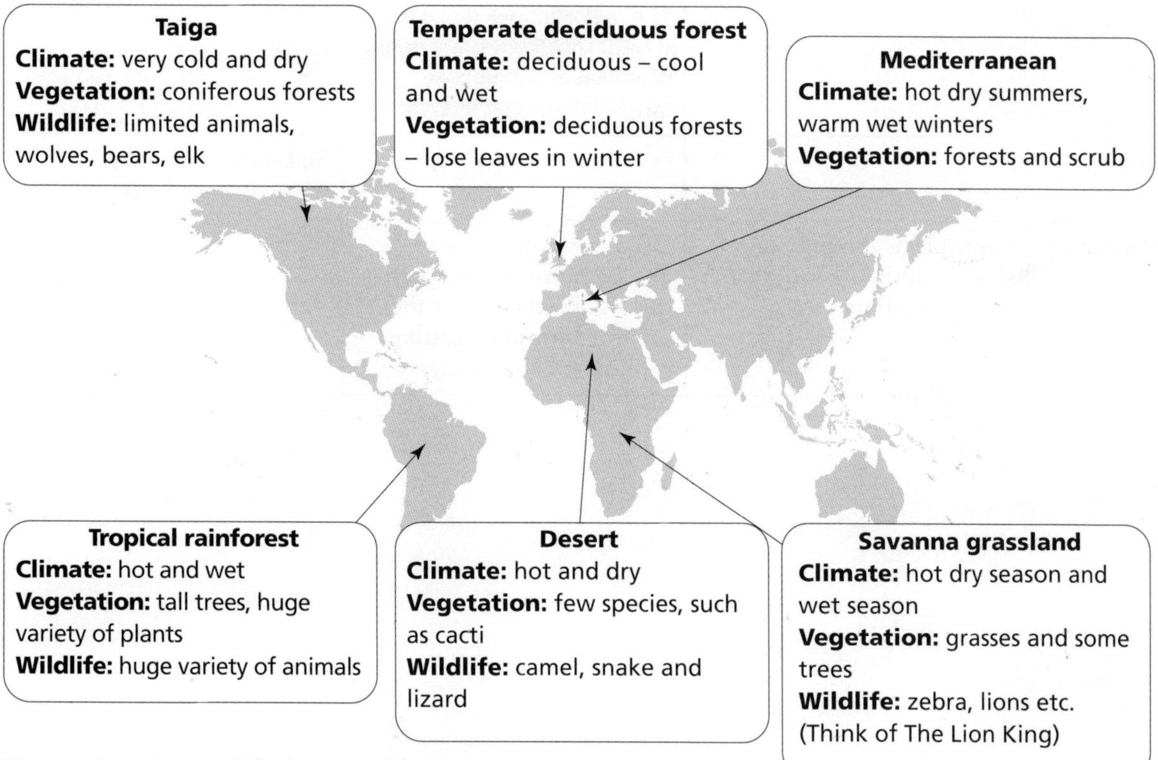

Taiga
Climate: very cold and dry
Vegetation: coniferous forests
Wildlife: limited animals, wolves, bears, elk

Temperate deciduous forest
Climate: deciduous – cool and wet
Vegetation: deciduous forests – lose leaves in winter

Mediterranean
Climate: hot dry summers, warm wet winters
Vegetation: forests and scrub

Tropical rainforest
Climate: hot and wet
Vegetation: tall trees, huge variety of plants
Wildlife: huge variety of animals

Desert
Climate: hot and dry
Vegetation: few species, such as cacti
Wildlife: camel, snake and lizard

Savanna grassland
Climate: hot dry season and wet season
Vegetation: grasses and some trees
Wildlife: zebra, lions etc. (Think of The Lion King)

Figure 4.1 A simplified map of biomes

Task 4.1

1 Copy Figure 4.1. Cut out the labels and try to stick them back on in the right places.
2 If you are a visual learner, imagine you are on a round the world trip in a low-flying plane. As you fly over each biome, look out of the window and imagine the climate, plants and animals.

Interaction between climate, soil and vegetation

You need to:
- know how climate, soil and vegetation affect each other for your local ecosystem and your tropical ecosystem
- understand how this could work in different ecosystems (at the higher tier).

General interactions between climate, soil and vegetation

	Climate	Soil	Vegetation
Climate		Rain goes into soil. Too much rain can wash away nutrients (**leaching**). Drought means water evaporates from soil leaving harmful salts behind Hot wet climates make rocks weather into soil quickly, and dead leaves decompose quickly making soil fertile	Rain is needed for growth, so is sunshine Frost can kill some plants, but helps others grow Hot wet climates lead to dead leaves decomposing quickly
Soil			Soil stores water and nutrients for plants
Vegetation	Large plants can provide shade and shelter for other plants to survive	Dead leaves decompose, putting nutrients back into the soil. Plants protect the soil from **erosion** – getting washed or blown away	

The table below shows us how this works for a local ecosystem.

Interactions between climate, soil and vegetation in the Big Wood Nature Reserve, Belvoir Park, Belfast

	Climate	Soil	Vegetation
Climate		800 mm rain means there is not much leaching. It is not hot (summer average 16 °C) so dead leaves decompose quite slowly – over about a year	The seasons make the trees deciduous – as it gets cooler in autumn they drop their leaves so they save energy during the winter There is plenty of rain for trees such as ash and oak to survive
Soil			Soil is quite fertile, so trees can get nutrients to grow
Vegetation	Wild flowers such as bluebell grow under the shelter of trees in spring, before they get too many leaves and make too much shadow	In autumn, dead leaves fall and are decomposed by insects such as the Forest Bug and bacteria. This puts lots of nutrients into the soil	

Task 4.2

Using the information in the boxes in Figure 4.2, try to make a table for the tropical rainforest, similar to above and on page 48. If you have studied tropical grassland instead, try using information from your notes to do the same thing.

Temperatures above 25°C and 1800 mm rain per year (heavy rain every afternoon) mean dead leaves etc. decompose very quickly and rock underneath the soil weathers quickly. Heavy rain may leach lots of nutrients away and wash soil away if there are no trees to protect it

High rainfall and temperatures mean lots of different plants, e.g. mahogany and ebony trees can grow (high **biodiversity**) and get very tall, about 40 m (high **biomass**). Lots of rain means trees have waxy leaves so water runs off instead of making them rot.

There are lots of dead leaves falling, providing nutrients to the soil. The plants hold the soil together and stop it washing away

Soil is deep but not very fertile as most nutrients get leached away by heavy rain. Most plants have shallow roots to get nutrients from the top layer of soil

Tall trees provide lots of shade, so not many plants grow on the ground. Some ferns grow here. Most other plants grow in clearings

Figure 4.2 Information boxes for interactions in the tropical rainforest

Food webs

You need to:
- *know what a food web is, including producers, consumers and decomposers*
- *know a few species for your local ecosystem and your tropical ecosystem.*

A food web illustrates the way in which energy is passed on within an ecosystem. Food webs can contain producers, consumers and decomposers. The arrows on a food web or chain show the direction in which the energy passes.

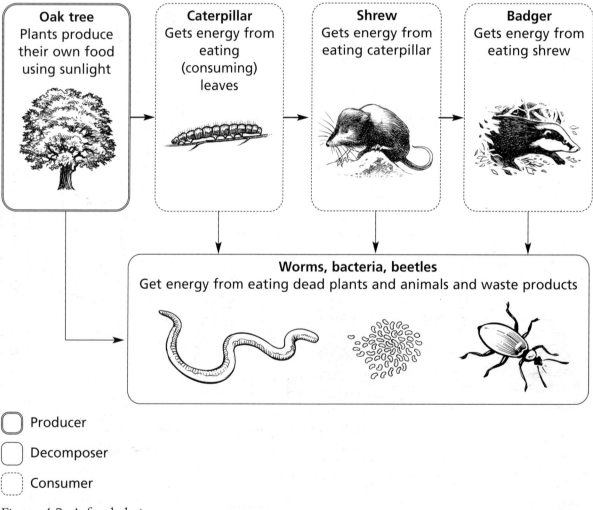

Oak tree	**Caterpillar**	**Shrew**	**Badger**
Plants produce their own food using sunlight	Gets energy from eating (consuming) leaves	Gets energy from eating caterpillar	Gets energy from eating shrew

Worms, bacteria, beetles
Get energy from eating dead plants and animals and waste products

◯ Producer

◯ Decomposer

⬚ Consumer

Figure 4.3 A food chain

This is a simple food chain. In most ecosystems there are lots of these which go together to make a food web.

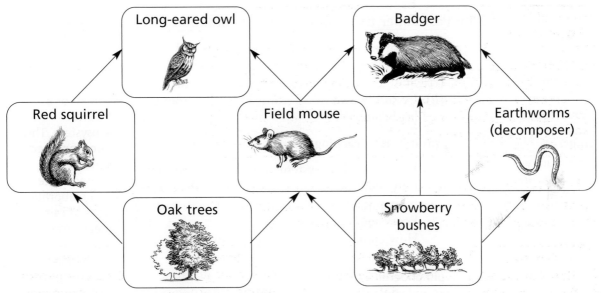

Figure 4.4 Food web for Big Wood Nature Reserve, Belvoir Park, Belfast

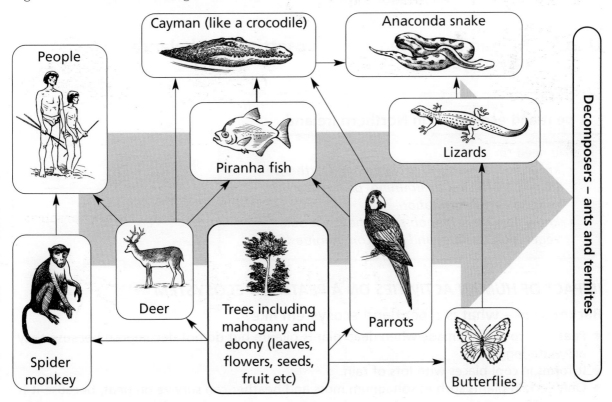

Figure 4.5 Food web for tropical rainforest in Brazil

Task 4.3

1 Label each of the species in the food webs in Figures 4.4 and 4.5 as producers or consumers.
2 Write out **two** food chains for each food web, starting with a producer each time and including at least two consumers.

You really need to learn definitions! This is worth 2 marks so you need to know it in full: 'a community of plants and animals and the environment they live in, including soil and climate'.

2006 Past Paper Exam Questions (Foundation Tier)

3 (a) Two elements of an ecosystem are plants and climate. Answer the questions which follow.
  (i) State the meaning of the term **ecosystem**. (2)
  (ii) Underline **two** other words for plants from the list below. (2)

  producers   leaching   vegetation   biome

  (iii) For a named ecosystem you have studied, state fully **one** way in which climate has affected the type of plants.
  Ecosystem (1)
  How climate has affected the plants (3)

You should underline producers and vegetation.

You should be able to name a small-scale ecosystem (such as Belvoir Forest) or a tropical ecosystem. This question needs statement, consequence and elaboration. 'Lots of rain means trees have waxy leaves so rain runs off instead of making them rot.'

Unit 2 – Human interference and upsetting the balance of ecosystems

A peatland ecosystem in Northern Ireland

You need to:
- know how a peatland ecosystem in Northern Ireland is affected by draining, peat extraction, grazing and afforestation
- know how conservation can benefit the soil, vegetation, animals and local communities.

IMPACT OF HUMAN ACTIVITIES ON A PEATLAND ECOSYSTEM

Background – what is a peatland ecosystem like?

◆ **Peat** is a type of soil made when dead plants pile up but do not decompose because they are waterlogged.
◆ It forms in cool places with lots of rain.
◆ Only certain plants such as sphagnum moss and heather can survive on peat, because it is wet and has very few nutrients.
◆ Peatlands are home for lots of insects (e.g. dragonflies), and other animals such as frogs, foxes and skylarks.

There are four main human activities affecting peatlands in Northern Ireland. The table on the following page shows how they have affected one peatland area – Cuilcagh Mountain, County Fermanagh.

Human activities affecting Cuilcagh Mountain

Human activity	Impact on soil	Impact on vegetation	Impact on animals
Draining – digging ditches to allow water to run out of soil into rivers. In the 1980s 14 km of drains were dug	Soil dries out	Specialist vegetation such as sphagnum moss and sundew are crowded out by other species which can now survive	Newts, frogs and insects lose their habitat
Peat extraction – local people have been digging peat for centuries, but on a small scale. In the 1980s mechanised cutting started	Soil is removed, and lower layers of peat are compacted	Vegetation is removed. No peat to support new vegetation growth	Loss of habitats
Grazing – some sheep can be supported in the peatland, but too many cause problems	Peat may be compacted by sheep trampling on it. If soil is left bare it may be eroded	Vegetation is removed	Lack of food and habitats for other animals
Afforestation – planting trees, usually conifers	Trees take water out of soil. Soil is fertilised, and fertiliser may be washed into other areas of the peatland	Heather moorland removed. Less light for other plants	Change of habitat

Task 4.4

Copy and complete the sketch below, labelling the four uses of the peatland at Cuilcagh Mountain. One has been done for you. For each one, write the impacts in the box. Use three different colours to show the impacts on soil, vegetation and animals.

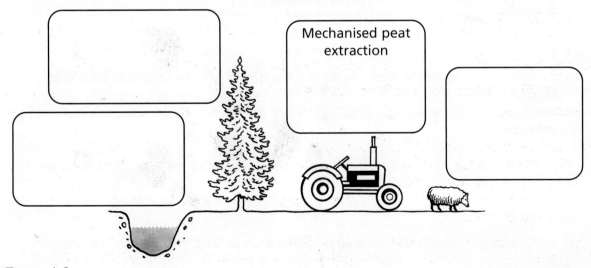

Mechanised peat extraction

Figure 4.6

Conservation of a peatland ecosystem

Conservation is the action taken to protect and improve an area for future use. To conserve the peatland ecosystem, Fermanagh District Council set up the Cuilcagh Mountain Park. This aims to:

◆ protect the peatland areas
◆ make people more aware of how important peatlands are.

To do this there has to be **management** of the peatland – this is the way it is looked after and used.

Actions taken	Benefits of action	Soil/vegetation/animals/local communities
The creation of an interpretative centre with information and café	Employment for 50 people	
Forestry Service have created a nature reserve for bog plants and animals, instead of planting trees	Natural vegetation remains, animals keep their habitat	
Farmers are not allowed to burn heather at certain times of year	Young animals are protected	
The area has been made an SSSI (Site of Special Scientific Interest)	Damage to vegetation and soil is illegal	
The area is part of an ESA (Environmentally Sensitive Area) Scheme	Farmers put fewer sheep to graze on the land, so heather is protected and soil is not compacted	
Small dams built to keep more water in the peat	Peatland stays wetter. Less water flows through Marble Arch Caves, so they can stay open more often and get more money from tourism	

Task 4.5
Copy the table and complete the third column to show who or what benefits from each action.

2006 Past Paper Exam Questions (Higher Tier)

3 **(d) (iii)** State **one** method of conserving peatland and outline a possible benefit of the measure.
Method (1)
Benefit (3)

This is not a case study question, so you don't have to be specific about one area. You can use your case study information to help you answer.

Method – could be stop cutting peat, or designate as an Environmentally Sensitive Area.

Benefit – you need one benefit, which you need to explain fully for 3 marks. 'Stop cutting peat so vegetation is not lost, meaning the animals do not lose their habitat and the whole ecosystem is protected.'

expand on answers like this!

A tropical ecosystem

You need to:
- know how a tropical ecosystem is affected by vegetation being cleared
- know how conservation can benefit the soil, vegetation, animals and local communities.

In this book we are dealing with tropical rainforests. You may have learnt about tropical grasslands. You only need to know one of them.

Impact of clearing vegetation in the Amazon Rainforest, South America
There are two ways vegetation is being cleared in the Amazon.

1 Slash and burn

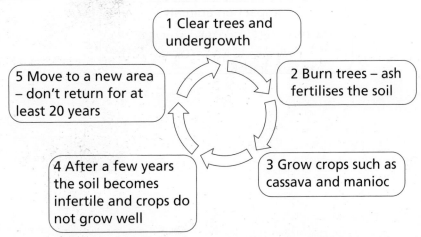

1 Clear trees and undergrowth

2 Burn trees – ash fertilises the soil

3 Grow crops such as cassava and manioc

4 After a few years the soil becomes infertile and crops do not grow well

5 Move to a new area – don't return for at least 20 years

Figure 4.7 Slash and burn – what happens

This is done by the Amerindians, who have lived in the Amazon rainforest for centuries. They clear a small area, farm it, then leave it to recover for a long time before returning to it.

This type of vegetation clearance is **sustainable** (can be carried out without permanent damage) because it allows the soil time to recover. All the impacts are short term or temporary.

◆ The soil temporarily loses its source of nutrients, but when vegetation grows back it recovers quickly. Some trees are always left to protect the soil from being washed away.
◆ The vegetation is mostly removed, but after a few years it quickly grows back, because the clearing is surrounded by plants which provide seeds for new plants to grow.
◆ The animals lose their habitat for a short while, but many will find food and shelter in the surrounding forest. The animals can return to the clearing after a few years.

Task 4.6

Copy and complete the boxes to show the impact on tropical rainforest of slash and burn farming.

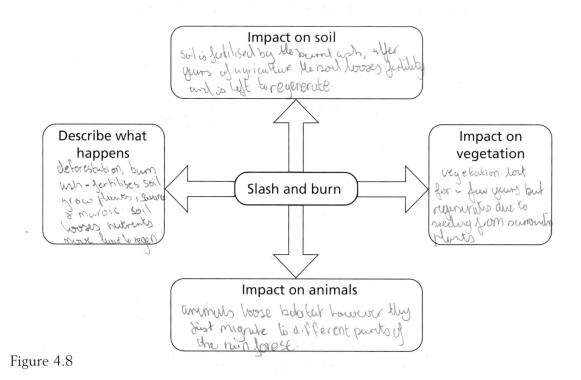

Impact on soil
Soil is fertilised by the burnt ash, after years of agriculture the soil looses fertility and is left to regenerate.

Describe what happens
deforestation, burn ash - fertilises soil grow plants, savanah & maroic soil looses nutrients more time to regen

Slash and burn

Impact on vegetation
vegetation lost for a few years but regenerates due to seeding from surrounding plants

Impact on animals
animals loose habitat however they first migrate to different parts of the rain forest.

Figure 4.8

2 Large-scale **deforestation** (cutting down trees)

This involves people clearing all the vegetation in large areas of the forest, using chainsaws, diggers and trucks. This is done for several reasons:

◆ to find valuable trees such as mahogany and rosewood to sell as timber
◆ to build new roads (the Trans-Amazonian Highway)
◆ to dig mines, such as the bauxite mine at Trombetas
◆ to build dams for hydroelectric power stations, such as the one at Tucurui
◆ to sell the land for cattle ranching
◆ to give farms to people from shanty towns.

The Brazilian Government is spending $45 billion on a scheme called Advance Brazil, which will clear large areas of Amazonia.

Large-scale deforestation has huge impacts on soil, vegetation and animals.

◆ The soil is left bare with nothing to protect it so it is washed away (eroded).
◆ The soil has no vegetation to give it nutrients, so it becomes infertile.
◆ The natural vegetation is removed from a large area. There are no nearby plants to provide seeds so it cannot grow back.
◆ The animals lose their habitat and food supply. So much forest is cleared that they cannot all find homes and food in the forest that remains.

This type of vegetation clearance is unsustainable – it cannot be continued forever – because too much damage is done, and the forest will eventually all be gone.

Task 4.7

Copy and complete the boxes to show the impacts of large-scale deforestation.

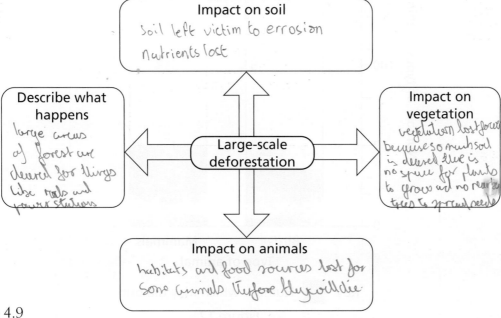

Impact on soil
Soil left victim to errosion
nutrients lost

Describe what happens
large areas of forest are cleared for things like roads and power stations

Large-scale deforestation

Impact on vegetation
vegetation lost forever because so much soil is cleared there is no space for plants to grow and no nearby trees to spread seeds

Impact on animals
habitats and food sources lost for some animals therefore they will die

Figure 4.9

Conservation of a tropical ecosystem

There are some efforts being made to conserve the rainforest:

◆ Brazil is committed to protecting 10 per cent of the rainforest in Brazil.
◆ Tumucumaque National Park is protected.
◆ In Peru the Manu Biosphere Reserve is protected – large areas cannot be cleared, lots of species cannot be hunted, and the local people have the right to live and work there.

Benefits of conservation:

◆ Soil – protected from erosion and keeps its source of nutrients.
◆ Vegetation – 1,600 plant species are protected, large areas cannot be cleared.
◆ Animals – 1000 bird species are protected.
◆ Local communities – can live and work in the area as they have always done, and can develop some sustainable economic activities such as using fruit and rubber trees.

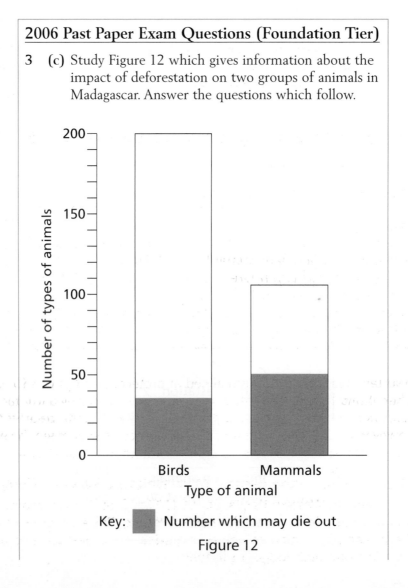

2006 Past Paper Exam Questions (Foundation Tier)

3 (c) Study Figure 12 which gives information about the impact of deforestation on two groups of animals in Madagascar. Answer the questions which follow.

Figure 12

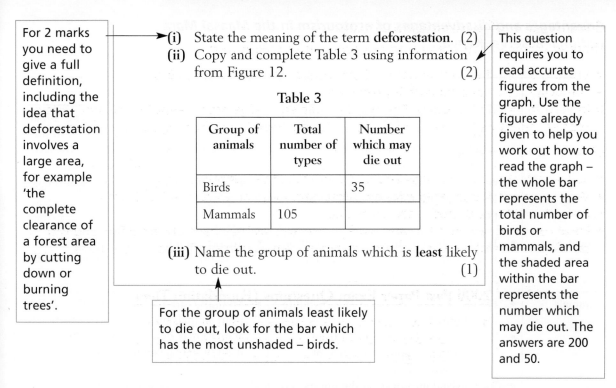

For 2 marks you need to give a full definition, including the idea that deforestation involves a large area, for example 'the complete clearance of a forest area by cutting down or burning trees'.

(i) State the meaning of the term **deforestation**. (2)
(ii) Copy and complete Table 3 using information from Figure 12. (2)

Table 3

Group of animals	Total number of types	Number which may die out
Birds		35
Mammals	105	

(iii) Name the group of animals which is **least** likely to die out. (1)

This question requires you to read accurate figures from the graph. Use the figures already given to help you work out how to read the graph – the whole bar represents the total number of birds or mammals, and the shaded area within the bar represents the number which may die out. The answers are 200 and 50.

For the group of animals least likely to die out, look for the bar which has the most unshaded – birds.

Unit 3 – Management of ecosystems and sustainable development

Advantages and disadvantages of ecotourism

You need to:
- *know what ecotourism is and how it can contribute to sustainable development in a tropical environment*
- *know place names, facts and figures for either a tropical rainforest or a tropical grassland case study*
- *know the advantages and/or disadvantages of ecotourism for local communities, vegetation, animals and soil.*

Ecotourism is a sustainable form of tourism aimed at protecting ecosystems for visitors to enjoy and also benefiting local communities. As well as environmental advantages, ecotourism should bring much needed employment and the education and health benefits that money can buy. It is, however, possible for some ecotourism businesses to damage the environment on which their livelihood is based because they are trying to maximise their income.

Case study of ecotourism – the Maasai Mara National Reserve, Kenya

Tourists visit this reserve in Western Kenya, about 150 km from Kenya's capital city, Nairobi, to see its abundant wildlife in a spectacular natural setting. The animals include lions, leopards, elephants and black rhino as well as migrating wildebeest and zebra. Tourist accommodation is in stone-built lodges or in tents.

Advantages and disadvantages of ecotourism in the Maasai Mara National Reserve, Kenya

	Advantages	Disadvantages
Local communities	• Employment as game wardens, guides, drivers, cooks, cleaners. The income supports extended families • Profits used to fund schools, health and community projects • Roads built for tourists benefit local people too	• Instead of woodcarving or dancing as part of their traditional culture, they now do it for cash, so their way of life has changed • Some employment is seasonal, leaving people unemployed for the rest of the year
Vegetation	• Profits from ecotourism can be spent on re-establishing natural grassland and maintaining vital habitats	• Tourist minibuses destroy grasses if they drive off the tracks to get closer to wildlife
Animals	• Patrols by game wardens reduce wildlife losses from poaching • The local people who benefit from ecotourism are more supportive of conservation measures • As grassland improves, so the numbers of grazing animals (e.g. zebra) increase and this attracts more predators (e.g. lions)	• Minibuses are meant to stay 25 m away from animals but not all do so. Some animals may be disturbed and prevented from drinking, eating or mating
Soil	• If minibuses stay on approved tracks there is less risk of soil erosion	• Soil erosion occurs where minibuses have gone off approved tracks and destroyed the vegetation cover

Task 4.8

Three, two, one!
For the Maasai Mara, or your own ecotourism case study, write down:

◆ three of the animals that tourists come to see
◆ two facts about the reserve/location visited
◆ one impact of ecotourism for each of the following: local communities, vegetation, animals and soil.

KNOWLEDGE TESTS

Knowledge Test I (Pages 47–52)

1 What is an ecosystem?
2 Name a biome (ecosystem at the global scale) with a very cold, dry climate, coniferous forests, wolves, bears and elk.
3 What vegetation and animals are typical of the Savanna biome?
4 What is the annual rainfall and summer temperature in Big Wood Nature Reserve, Belvoir Park, Belfast?
5 Name two tree species, one wildflower and one insect found in Big Wood Nature Reserve.
6 What annual rainfall and temperature are typical of tropical rainforests?
7 Name two tree species found in tropical rainforests.
8 What is the impact of heavy rainfall on tropical rainforest soils?
9 In a food chain, what are plants that produce their own food using sunlight known as?
10 How does a food web differ from a food chain?

KNOWLEDGE TESTS

Knowledge Test II (Pages 52–59)

1 List three human activities which affect peatlands in Northern Ireland.
2 Name two plant species which thrive in the waterlogged, low-nutrient conditions of a peatland ecosystem.
3 What length of drainage ditches was dug on Cuilcagh Mountain in the 1980s?
4 What is the impact of overgrazing by sheep on peatlands?
5 Cuilcagh Mountain is an SSSI and part of an ESA. What do these initials stand for?
6 Name a sustainable method of cultivation used by Amerindians in the Amazon rainforest for centuries.
7 Name the $45 billion Brazilian Government scheme to clear large areas of Amazonia for roads, mining and cattle-ranching.
8 What is the impact on animals of large-scale deforestation in rainforests?
9 What percentage of rainforest has Brazil promised to protect?
10 How does conservation of tropical rainforest benefit local communities?

KNOWLEDGE TESTS

Knowledge Test III (Pages 59–60)

1 What is ecotourism?
2 Describe the location of the Maasai Mara National Reserve.
3 Describe tourist accommodation in the Maasai Mara.
4 What types of jobs in ecotourism are available to local people?
5 What is a disadvantage of such employment?
6 What benefit can ecotourism bring for local health and education?
7 What negative impact can tourist minibuses have on vegetation and soil?
8 What is the minimum distance that minibuses should keep from animals?

Chapter 5

THEME D: POPULATION AND RESOURCES

Unit 1 – Distribution and density

Physical and economic factors affecting distribution and density

You need to:
- *know what population distribution and density are*
- *be able to explain why two areas of the world have high population density and two areas have low density*
- *understand the physical and economic factors that explain the population distribution and density of one country within the European Union.*

Population distribution is the way in which people are spread out across the earth's surface. This is uneven, with some areas crowded and other areas sparsely populated.

Population density is the number of people living in a given area, usually 1 km². It is found by dividing the total population of a country or region by its area.

Taking Spain as an example:

Total population = 39.7 million
Area = 499,000 km²

$$\text{Density} = \frac{39,700,000}{499,000}$$

= 79.6 persons per km²

The physical factors that affect population density and distribution are concerned with the natural environment, that is relief (mountains, valleys and plains), climate, water supply, soils and vegetation.

The economic factors are concerned with money and making a living.

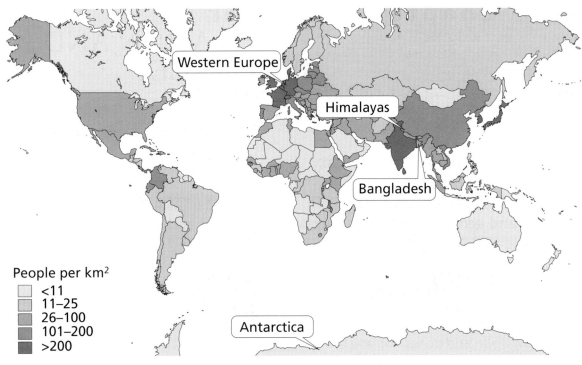

Figure 5.1 World map of population density

People per km²
- <11
- 11–25
- 26–100
- 101–200
- >200

The global pattern of population distribution and density

Area	Density	Physical factors	Economic factors
Antarctica	Low	• Extremely cold climate with winter temperatures below −50°C so everyday activities are very difficult • Permanent ice cover so soils and vegetation do not develop	• No farming possible • Exploration for other resources, e.g. minerals, is strictly controlled by international agreement • Only research scientists live there
Himalayas	Low	• Extremely cold climate at high altitudes • Thin soils on steep slopes • Little flat land for growing crops	• Poor transport links because road building is extremely difficult on very steep slopes
Bangladesh	High	• Flat land • Deep rich soils deposited by rivers • Tropical high temperatures and monsoon rainfall	• Rice farming with up to three crops per year supports many subsistence farmers • Good transport links
Western Europe	High	• Large areas of lowland with fertile soil for farming • No extremes of climate (temperate) so comfortable environment to live in	• Good road and rail links easily built across lowlands • Coal and iron ore reserves providing resources for manufacturing industry

Task 5.1

Take each of the four locations named on Figure 5.1 in turn and from memory try to list the physical and economic factors that explain their high or low population density.

Case study of population distribution and density in Spain

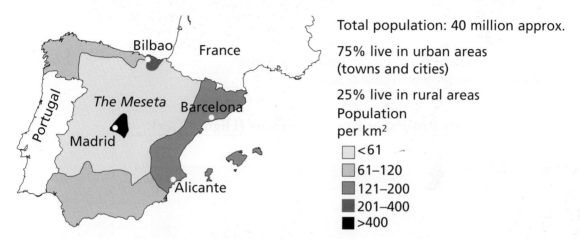

Total population: 40 million approx.

75% live in urban areas
(towns and cities)

25% live in rural areas
Population
per km²

<table>
<tr><td>☐</td><td><61</td></tr>
<tr><td>☐</td><td>61–120</td></tr>
<tr><td>☐</td><td>121–200</td></tr>
<tr><td>☐</td><td>201–400</td></tr>
<tr><td>■</td><td>>400</td></tr>
</table>

Figure 5.2 Population density map of Spain

The population of Spain is unevenly distributed. The most densely populated areas are around the capital, Madrid, and in the Basque Country around Bilbao in the north. The east coast, from Barcelona south to Alicante, has a fairly high population density. The least densely populated region is the central plain known as the Meseta. This pattern can be explained in terms of physical and economic factors. *Case Study*

Physical factors		Economic factors
Climate	Relief	
• The climate of the Meseta is influenced by **continentality** (i.e. distance from the sea). It has hot, dry summers and cold, dry winters and so is suited only to wheat farming, sheep, goats and some vineyards. The yields are low and few people are employed so population density is low • The east coast has hot, dry, sunny summers which attract tourists to its beaches. Tourism creates jobs and supports other businesses in the region, helping to explain the above average population density	• The mountainous regions (e.g. the Pyrenees along the border with France) have steep slopes, poor accessibility and cold winters so these areas have a low population density	• Madrid (pop. 3 million) is the capital and therefore has attracted people to fill jobs in government offices, finance, business and services. It is also an important centre for manufacturing • Barcelona (pop. 1.8 million) is the second largest city and chief port, with many jobs in industry and commerce. Barcelona is also an important tourist destination • Bilbao (pop. 0.4 million) has a steel industry, based on local iron ore resources, as well as jobs in electronics and IT These three areas are the richest in Spain and their economic activities explain their high population densities

Task 5.2

1 Draw a spider diagram to show the physical and economic factors that influence the population distribution of Spain, adding symbols where possible to help you to visualise the information. Include two place names and two figures. If you have studied population distribution in a different EU country, try to produce a similar diagram for it.

2 Three, two, one!
Give the name of:

- ◆ three cities in Spain
- ◆ two physical factors that help to explain population density
- ◆ one sparsely populated region in central Spain.

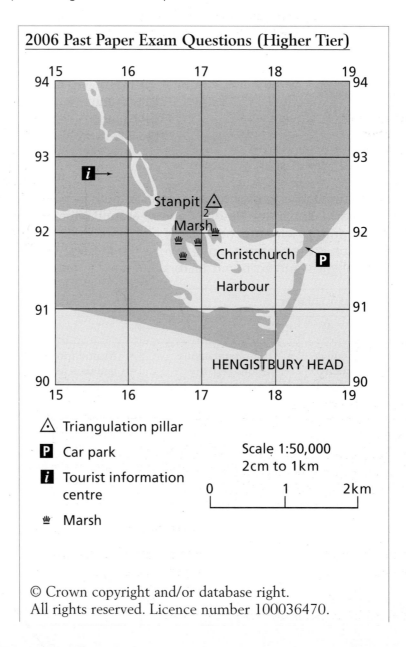

2006 Past Paper Exam Questions (Higher Tier)

Stanpit
Marsh
Christchurch
Harbour

HENGISTBURY HEAD

△ Triangulation pillar

P Car park

i Tourist information centre

♨ Marsh

Scale 1:50,000
2cm to 1km

0   1   2km

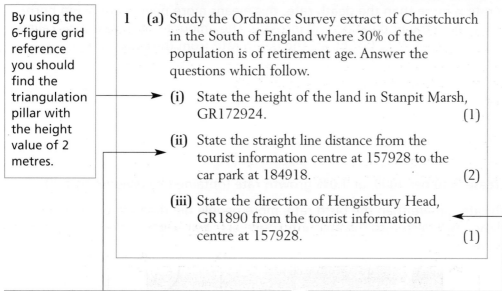

By using the 6-figure grid reference you should find the triangulation pillar with the height value of 2 metres.

1 (a) Study the Ordnance Survey extract of Christchurch in the South of England where 30% of the population is of retirement age. Answer the questions which follow.

(i) State the height of the land in Stanpit Marsh, GR172924. (1)

(ii) State the straight line distance from the tourist information centre at 157928 to the car park at 184918. (2)

(iii) State the direction of Hengistbury Head, GR1890 from the tourist information centre at 157928. (1)

First, use the grid references to find the car park and information centre. As in both cases there is an arrow from the symbol to the location of the feature it is important to measure the distance in centimetres between the arrowheads, not the symbols. This is 5.8 cm and using the scale you can divide by two to find the distance is 2.9 km. There are 2 marks for an accurate answer of 2.8–3.0 km and 1 mark for the less accurate answers 2.7–2.79 or 3.01–3.1 km.

Note the question asks what is the direction of Hengistbury Head from the information centre. Imagine yourself standing at the information centre. What direction do you travel in order to reach Hengistbury Head? The answer is south east. Don't be tempted by more complicated answers such as SSE or ESE. The direction questions only have answers of N, NE, E, SE, S, SW, W or NW.

Unit 2 – Population changes over time

Global population change

You need to:
- *know what is meant by birth rate and death rate*
- *know how birth rates, death rates and the population of the world have changed since 1700.*

Birth rate is:

◆ the number of live births
◆ per 1000 people
◆ per year.

Death rate is:

◆ the number of deaths
◆ per 1000 people
◆ per year.

Try to remember all three parts of these definitions!

When the birth rate is more than the death rate, this means more people are being born than dying in any year so the population will increase. The amount it increases by is called the natural increase. To work it out, subtract the death rate from the birth rate.

Example:

Birth rate   = 30
Death rate   = 20

Natural increase = 30 – 20
                     = 10

The natural increase is 10 per 1000, or 1.0% growth rate (obtained by dividing by ten).

When the death rate is more than the birth rate, more people die than are born in any year. The population will decrease. The amount it decreases by can be worked out in the same way as above.

Example:

Birth rate   = 20
Death rate   = 25

Natural increase = 20 – 25
                     = –5

The natural increase is –5 per 1000, or –0.5% growth rate.

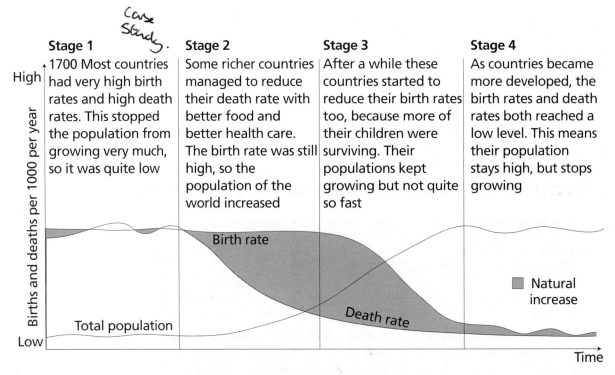

Figure 5.3 Changes in birth rate, death rate and world population

The population of the whole world has been affected by the changes shown on Figure 5.3.

In more developed countries, such as the UK and USA, the populations have already increased and now stay more or less the same.

Some less developed countries such as India and Mexico are now in the middle stages shown on Figure 5.3, and their populations are growing quickly.

This means the world population is going to grow a lot more in the next few years.

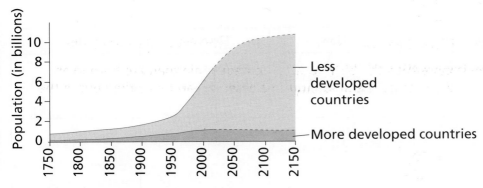

Figure 5. 4 Graph of world population growth

Task 5.3
Using Figure 5.4 decide which statements are true and which are false.

1 The population of the world is decreasing. F
2 The population of the world is increasing. T
3 World population grew slowly until 1950. T
4 World population grew rapidly from 1750 F
5 World population grew rapidly from 1950. T
6 The population in 2000 was growing fastest in MEDCs. F
7 The population in LEDCs is growing much faster than in MEDCs. T
8 LEDCs are mostly in the middle stages of Figure 5.3. T
9 LEDCs are mostly in the last stage of Figure 5.3. F

TWO CASE STUDIES OF POPULATION CHANGE AND STRUCTURE

Population change

You need to:
- *know about population change and structure in a LEDC and a MEDC*
- *know about changes in birth and death rates, including reasons, and changes in migration.*

Birth rate and death rate are affected by lots of different factors. Try the task below.

Task 5.4

Put the factors from the box in the correct increase or decrease section of the table. Then fill in the 'how' columns.

> Clean water   Sewage system   Reliable contraception   Good hospitals   Good food
> People getting married later   Children needed to work   Vaccinations   Lots of elderly people

Affects	Increase	How	Decrease	How
Birth rate	Children need to work	parents need children for support when they are old or to carry on family businesses	Reliable contraception, Good hospitals, clean water, people get married later	less accidents, less infant mortality, less disease & infection, people decide too old
Death rate	Lots of elderly people	More deaths as people die of natural causes.	The same as above apart from 1 & 4. Sewage system and Vaccinations	helps contain disease and sewage systems provide hygiene.

We have summarised Italy (MEDC) and Mexico (LEDC) here. If you have a different case study, try to produce a table like the one below using your case study details. This will help to make sure you learn the key points. *Case Study*

	Italy (MEDC)	Mexico (LEDC)
Birth rate change	Now very low. Decreased from 16 in 1970s to 9 in 1990s	Still quite high. Decreased from 43 in 1970s to 25 in 1990s
Reasons	More women going out to work, most children surviving, people getting married later	Mexico is becoming more developed and more children are now surviving, so the birth rate has decreased a bit. There are still lots of people of the right age to have a family so the figure is still quite high
Death rate change	Increased slightly from 9.8 in 1970s to 10.4 in 1990s	Decreased from 9 in 1970s to 5 in 1990s
Reasons	Every 1000 people now includes more elderly people, so therefore more are dying	Better health care has reduced deaths. Every 1000 people now includes more young people, so fewer of these are dying
Migration	For a long while people from the South went to other European countries to earn money. Now this is less common, and people are migrating into Italy from Eastern Europe	Large numbers of people cross the border to the USA, often illegally, to earn money
Total population change	Increasing slowly – 0.6% in 1970s but only 0.1% in 1990s. Soon the population may begin to fall	Increasing rapidly, though not as fast as before – 3% growth in 1970s, only 1.6% in 1990s

Population structure and pyramids, and impacts of population change

You need to:
- *know about population pyramids including dependency, and the impacts of youth dependency and aged dependency*
- *be able to interpret population pyramids.*

Population structure, or **composition**, is the way the population is divided between male and female, and different age groups.

It can be shown clearly on a population pyramid such as Figure 5.6.

Task 5.5

Match up the numbered labels to the appropriate letters on the pyramids.

1 Wide base shows high birth rate *e*
2 Narrow base shows low birth rate *b*
3 Straight pyramid shows low death rate *a*
4 Triangular pyramid shows high death rate *d*
5 Tall pyramid shows high life expectancy *h*
6 Short pyramid shows low life expectancy *c*
7 Missing males in 20s and 30s shows out-migration *f*
8 Extra males in 20s and 30s shows in-migration *g*

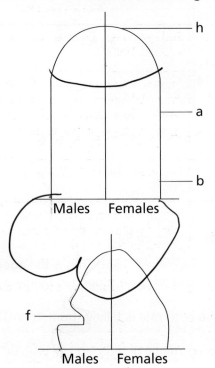

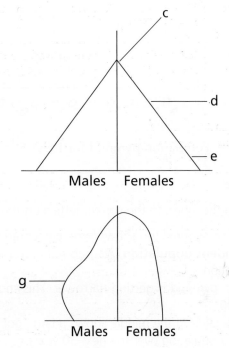

Figure 5.5 Population pyramids

Dependency can be seen clearly on population pyramids.

There are two groups of people who are dependent on the people who are of working age to support them:

a Aged dependent – age 65+

b Youth dependent – age 0–14

We can calculate a dependency ratio to show the percentage of the population dependent on the rest.

$$\text{Dependency ratio} = \frac{\text{youth dependent} + \text{aged dependent}}{\text{working population}} \times 100$$

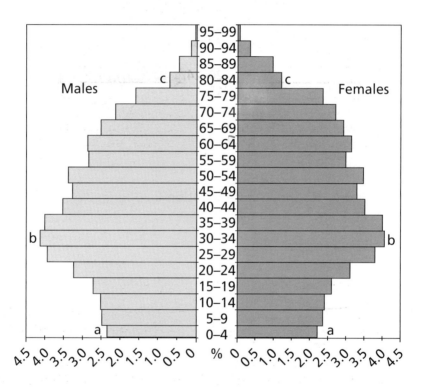

Figure 5.6 Population pyramid for Italy

Task 5.6

Match up the labels to the correct letters on the pyramid in Figure 5.6.

1 Width of pyramid top shows large percentage of elderly people (18%). This is the **aged dependent population,** who do not earn money and need to be supported by the working population. C

2 Base of pyramid is getting narrower. This shows the birth rate is falling (from 16 in 1970s to 9 in 2000). a

3 Wide section in the middle shows a large population currently of working age who will add to elderly population over the next 30 years. b

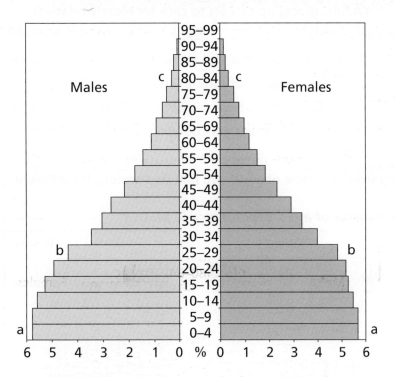

Figure 5.7 Population pyramid for Mexico

Task 5.7

Match up the labels with the correct letters on the pyramid in Figure 5.7.

1 Base of pyramid is getting wider. This shows the birth rate is high (25 in 1995–2000). This is the **youth dependent** population, who do not earn money and need to be supported by the working population. a
2 Lots of people of childbearing age means the birth rate will stay high. b
3 Tall pyramid shows the death rate is going down (9 in 1970, 5 in 2000) so there will be more elderly people to be provided for. c

Both aged dependency and youth dependency create problems for the country to deal with. The government gets money by taxing people on what they earn. This means people of working age are needed to provide tax money to pay for services such as health care, education and so on. This creates economic impacts (to do with money). There are also social impacts (to do with the way people behave).

Task 5.8

Copy and complete the tables on the following page by putting the impacts from the box into the correct parts of the tables. Make sure you can explain your decisions. Some may fit into more than one part of the table!

Adults giving up careers to care for elderly relatives
Elderly can provide wise advice   Expensive health care for the elderly
Lack of school buildings and facilities   Lack of teachers
Large numbers of infant vaccinations needed
Lots of young adults entering the labour market   Meals on wheels and home helps
Pensions   Relatives may be able to provide childcare
Residential homes needed   Strain on carers
Strain on primary schools – some operate two half-day sessions for different groups of pupils

Socio-economic impacts of aged dependency in MEDCs

	Costs	Benefits
Social	• adults give up careers	• elderly can provide wise advice
Economic	• Elderly need expensive hospitals • Pensions • Residential homes needed	Meals on wheels and home helps

Socio-economic impacts of youth dependency in LEDCs

	Costs	Benefits
Social	•	
Economic	• lack of school buildings	• lots of adults enter labour market

2006 Past Paper Exam Questions (Higher Tier)

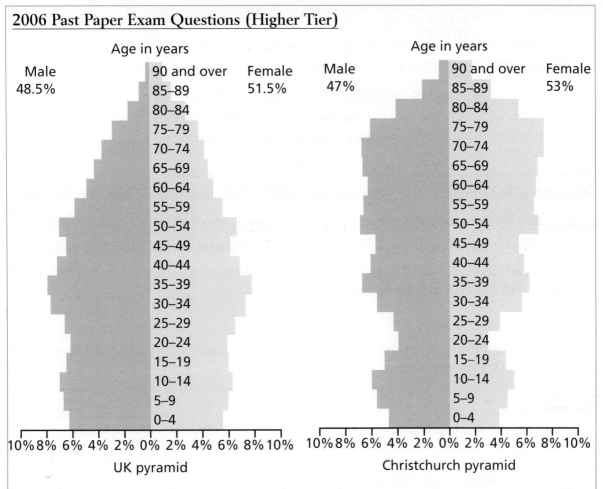

UK pyramid

Christchurch pyramid

(b) Study Figure 1 which shows the population pyramids for the UK and for Christchurch in 2001. Answer the questions which follow.

(ii) State fully **two** differences between the population structure for Christchurch and the UK. (6)

(iii) State fully **one** disadvantage to a country of having a large aged dependent population. (3)

Decide first on the two differences you will put in your answer, then try to write 3 marks' worth for each. This is a graph so you will be rewarded for referring to it or quoting figures from it. A valid answer would be 'Christchurch has a greater proportion of old people aged over 65 than the UK as Christchurch's pyramid looks top-heavy' or 'The percentage of young people aged 0–29 in Christchurch is smaller than for the UK as a whole, e.g. on the UK pyramid 0–4 year olds are about 6% but in Christchurch they are only about 4% for both males and females.' Note that no explanation is required.

Think of one idea and expand on it, using the statement, consequence and elaboration format:

- 'Old people are more likely to fall ill
- so more hospitals need to be built
- and the Government has to find money to pay for this through increasing taxes.'

International migration

You need to:
- know about the positive and negative impacts of international migration, including how it affects your case studies
- know about the challenges and opportunities of multicultural societies.

Migration is when people move house permanently. People who migrate are called migrants.

Immigration is when people move into a country. People who do this are called immigrants.

Emigration is when people move out of a country. People who do this are called emigrants.

Migration can have positive or negative impacts on the country people leave, the country they go to and the migrants themselves.

Task 5.9

The table below shows impacts of migration. For each, decide whether it is positive or negative, and write a + or − in the last column.

Impact on	Impact	+ or −
The country people leave	Lose best qualified people (e.g. the brain drain from Northern Ireland to Britain and North America)	−
	Fewer people to provide for	+
	Emigrants may send money back	+
The country people go to	More people to provide housing, health care, education etc. for	−
	More people to work and earn money	+ x −
	Migrants may bring in important skills	+ > −
	Migrants may be willing to work for low wages (e.g. food processing plants in Dungannon use migrant workers from Portugal)	+
	Migrants may take jobs away from local people, which may lead to racial tension	−
The migrants	May get good job, be able to send money home	+
	May be lonely, unable to speak the language	−
	May find cultural differences difficult	−
	May be eligible for benefits	+
	May get better health care and education than at home	+

A **multicultural society** is a society containing people from different cultures, races, religions, languages or nationalities. Britain is a multicultural society, with many people from the Caribbean and different parts of Asia. Northern Ireland is becoming more multicultural.

This kind of society has many challenges and opportunities.

Challenges and opportunities of a multicultural society

Challenges	Opportunities
• Racial discrimination and tensions • Language difficulties • Fear, intolerance • Residential segregation – immigrants often live near each other for protection or to set up services they need like specialist shops or places of worship	• Different foods – e.g. Chinese and Indian restaurants • Music from different cultures • Festivals – Notting Hill Carnival started as a celebration of West Indian culture • Variety of cultures, religions etc. broadens people's experiences

Task 5.10

The following statements are about things that could happen in a multicultural society. Decide whether each one counts as a challenge or an opportunity or both, and explain why.

a *The Kumars at No. 42* has become a very popular TV show. Opportunity

b The Smith family are arguing about whether to go for Chinese, Indian or Thai takeaway on Saturday night. Opportunity

c Mohammed is bullied at school because he doesn't go to assembly and has darker skin than the rest of his class. Challenge

d The area of Manningham in Bradford has many mosques, temples, Islamic schools, halal butchers and shops where you can buy saris and hijaab clothes. Opportunity

e Primary school children learn Indian dancing as well as Scottish or Irish dancing. Opportunity

f Secondary pupils can study for GCSEs in languages such as Chinese, Urdu and Gujarati. Opportunity

g The elderly couple, Mr and Mrs Jones, are now the only white couple living in their street. Challenge

Unit 3 – Population growth and sustainability

Overpopulation

You need to:
- *know what is meant by overpopulation*
- *know what causes it*
- *know what impacts it has*
- *understand that we need to find a balance between population and using oil as energy.*

Wherever people live they need things such as:

◆ water
◆ land to grow crops
◆ something to build shelter with
◆ fuel for cooking and keeping warm.

These are just the essentials. In modern societies there are other things such as transport systems and education. Things which people can use, such as the things listed on the previous page, are called **resources**.

Within an area there are a certain number of resources. They can support a certain number of people until there is no longer enough to go round. If there are too many people for the resources to support them at an adequate standard of living, this is called **overpopulation**. If there are not enough people to use the resources effectively, this is called **underpopulation.**

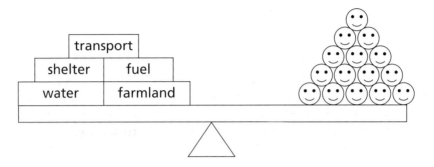

Figure 5.8 The balance between population and resources

Causes of overpopulation

Figure 5.8 shows how there needs to be a balance between population and resources. If population increases too much, the see-saw will tip. If resources decrease too much, the see-saw will also tip. This shows that overpopulation can be caused by three things:

◆ population growth
◆ lack of resources
◆ resource depletion (using them up).

Task 5.11

1 Make a list of resources which you have used today such as transport and food. Think about the resources which were used to create the things you use – such as wood to make paper, or coal to make electricity.
2 Look at Figures 5.9a and 5.9b. Which shows overpopulation, and which shows underpopulation?

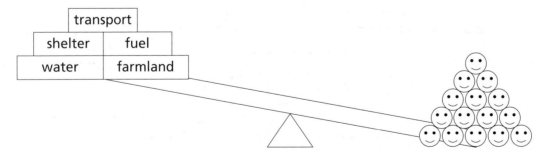

Figure 5.9a

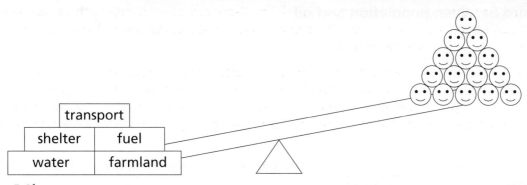

Figure 5.9b

Resource depletion is when people use resources up. Some resources are renewable, so they cannot be used up (such as wind for wind power, sunshine for solar power). But we use up non-renewable resources such as oil, coal, clean water supplies and good soil for farming. This may be because a bigger population needs more resources to survive, or because they use more resources to raise their standard of living (e.g. everyone wants TVs and mobile phones).

Impacts of overpopulation

Overpopulation has very different impacts in different parts of the world.

For example:

◆ Too many people letting their animals graze in an area will mean all the plants are eaten, and the soil is left bare, and is eroded by water and wind. It can no longer support farming. This has happened in the Sahel region of Africa, for example in Mali. It can cause famines where people starve because they haven't got enough food.
◆ Too many people living in cities in MEDCs, such as London, make them very crowded. Transport systems cannot cope, and people live in polluted noisy environments. This reduces people's quality of life.

Task 5.12

Copy and complete the spider diagram below.

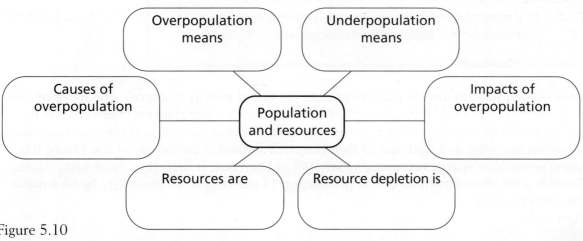

Figure 5.10

Balance between population and oil

Oil is used for:

◆ petrol and diesel for cars, lorries, trains, ships, planes etc.
◆ making plastics
◆ heating systems.

As population increases, and as LEDCs such as India become wealthier and more people want cars, more oil will be needed.

This is not sustainable – oil will run out one day. Some people think it will run out in about 50 years.

There are other problems with using oil which make it unsustainable:

◆ Burning oil produces carbon dioxide which contributes to global warming, and sulphur dioxide, which contributes to acid rain.
◆ When there is an oil spill in the sea, the oil pollutes the sea, killing animals and birds.
◆ Lots of oil is found in countries which are politically unstable. Prices can suddenly rise because of political problems. Wars such as the Gulf War may be partly because of oil prices.

We need to find a balance between population and oil use. There are several ways of doing this:

◆ reduce the population
◆ reduce the amount of oil we use
◆ find alternatives to oil such as wind power, solar power, recycled plastic, plastics made from plants.

Sustainable approaches to energy use: renewable energy

You need to:
* *know case study details of one renewable energy production scheme on a regional or national scale, in particular:*
  * *benefits and problems for the environment*
  * *benefits for sustainable development.*

Coal, oil and natural gas are non-renewable (or finite) energy resources. The more of them that are extracted from the earth and used, the fewer energy reserves there are left for use by future generations. This is not sustainable. Burning coal, oil and gas also contributes to global warming and acid rain so that the environment is damaged for the future too. Using renewable energy resources, which will not run out, is therefore more sustainable. There is a UK government target of generating 15 per cent of all electricity by renewable methods by 2015.

Task 5.13

1 Copy and complete the following sentences by selecting the correct energy resource from the word box below.
a _____ collects energy from sunlight using solar panels.
b _____ is made by harnessing the power of running water.
c _____ is turned into electricity using wind turbines.
d _____ makes use of natural heat from under the earth, usually in volcanic regions.
e _____ makes use of the sea's energy as it moves in and out of an estuary twice daily.

| Tidal energy | Hydroelectric power (HEP) |
| Geothermal energy | Solar energy | Wind energy |

2 Name an energy resource obtained from the sea, other than tidal energy.

Case study of wind power in Northern Ireland

Northern Ireland has nine wind farms, located on hilltops in upland areas where wind speeds are high and reliable. Each wind farm has between 10 and 20 wind turbines, painted grey so that they look less visible against the sky. Examples include Corkey on the Antrim Plateau and Lendrum's Bridge in Co Tyrone.

Potential for sustainable development:

◆ To be sustainable, energy has to be produced without wasting non-renewable resources or damaging the environment.
◆ As wind energy is renewable it conserves our reserves of fossil fuels for the future.
◆ Using wind energy means that less coal, oil and gas is burned in power stations so the atmosphere will contain lower levels of greenhouse gases which cause global warming.

However, all the wind farms in Northern Ireland contribute less than 2 per cent of the electricity used in Northern Ireland. As they cannot generate electricity during either calm or very stormy conditions, we will continue to rely on power stations for the majority of our energy needs. This means that wind energy makes a small but valuable contribution to sustainability.

Impact on the environment

Benefits for the environment	Problems for the environment
• No carbon dioxide (CO_2) emissions so no contribution to global warming • No sulphur dioxide (SO_2) emissions so no contribution to acid rain • Minimal disruption to surrounding peatland habitat • The RSPB says that wind farms, appropriately located, pose no significant hazard to birds. As climate change is the most serious long-term threat to wildlife in Britain, reduction in use of fossil fuels will benefit wildlife	• Visual pollution. Wind farms are situated on hilltops, visible for miles around and so can be regarded as eyesores • Noise pollution. Although few people live nearby, local residents may find the noise of the rotating blades disruptive • Poorly sited wind farms can harm birds by loss of habitat, disruption of feeding and breeding or collision with rotor blades

KNOWLEDGE TESTS

Knowledge Test I (Pages 63–67)

1 Select from the following list two areas of high population density: Antarctica, Himalayas, Bangladesh, Western Europe.
2 Why does Bangladesh have deep, rich soils?
3 What type of farming supports the majority of Bangladesh's population?
4 What is the total population of Spain, and the percentage who live in towns and cities?
5 Name the least densely populated area of Spain.
6 Why does this region have cold, dry winters and hot, dry summers?
7 Name a mountain area with low population density, on the border between France and Spain.
8 How does climate help to explain the above average population density of the east coast of Spain?
9 What is the name and population of the capital city of Spain?
10 Name two other major Spanish cities.

KNOWLEDGE TESTS

Knowledge Test II (Pages 67–77)

1 When birth rate is much greater than death rate, does the population grow rapidly, grow slowly or decrease?
2 When birth rate is slightly less than death rate, does the population grow rapidly, grow slowly or decrease?
3 What is the impact on birth rate of women going to work?
4 What is the impact on birth rate of low infant mortality?
5 Which country, Italy or Mexico, had 3% population growth in the 1970s but only 1.6% in the 1990s?
6 What age groups are defined as (a) youth dependent (b) aged dependent?
7 What type of dependent population results in shortage of school buildings and teachers?
8 What is an emigrant?
9 How might migration have a positive impact for the country the migrants move to?
10 State one challenge that may arise in multicultural societies.

KNOWLEDGE TESTS

Knowledge Test III (Pages 77–81)

1 What word is used for the things that people need, such as water, land, building materials and fuel?

2 Copy and complete the following sentence correctly. Overpopulation occurs if there are too many people for the resources to support them at _____

3 What, apart from population growth, can cause overpopulation?

4 What is the impact of overpopulation in the countries of the Sahel, such as Mali?

5 State three non-renewable (finite) energy resources.

6 State three renewable sources of energy.

7 Name a wind farm location in Northern Ireland.

8 What percentage of Northern Ireland's electricity do its nine wind farms generate?

9 State two reasons why wind farms are good for the environment.

10 State two reasons why nearby residents might object to the building of a wind farm.

Chapter 6 THEME E: ECONOMIC CHANGE AND DEVELOPMENT

Unit 1 – Economic change creates new opportunities

Economic activity

You need to:
- *know definitions and examples of primary, secondary and tertiary industries.*

An economic activity is any job or industry that makes money. There are three main categories:

- **Primary industries** obtain raw materials by extracting them from the earth or sea. They include farming, fishing, forestry, quarrying and mining.

- **Secondary industries** manufacture a product. They may use the raw materials from primary industry (e.g. furniture making) or may assemble components made by other secondary industries (e.g. car assembly).

- **Tertiary industries** provide a service to people or to businesses (e.g. health, advertising, transport and retailing).

Task 6.1

Place each of the following jobs in the correct column of your own copy of the table below.

Hotel manager   Trawler fisherman   Civil servant   Shipyard worker   Dressmaker
Insurance salesman   Coal miner   Travel agent   Glass blower

Primary	Secondary	Tertiary
Coal miner	Shipyard worker	Hotel
Trawler	Dress maker	civil servant
	glass blower	Sh insurance
		travel agent

Change in function of industrial premises

You need to:
- *know that economic change occurs and creates new opportunities*
- *know a case study of change in function of industrial premises, bringing advantages to people and the economy.*

As economic change happens over time, the proportion of people working in each category also changes. In Northern Ireland, employment in primary activities is very small (less than 2.5 per cent), manufacturing (secondary) employment is declining and tertiary employment is increasing. This means that there are old factory buildings, no longer used for manufacturing, for which a new use or function has to be found.

Case study

✳ Case study of change in function of industrial premises – Yorkgate, Belfast

Location: a 5-hectare site on York Street, less than 1 km north of Belfast's Central Business District (CBD)

Formerly: Gallaher's Tobacco factory, until it closed in 1988

- ◆ a traditional industry, located close to Belfast docks where raw materials were imported
- ◆ employed 1000 people in secondary manufacturing jobs
- ◆ closed because of decline in UK market as many people gave up smoking, and cheaper production in LEDCs where the market is expanding.

New function: Retail and leisure complex. Services offered include Movie House multiplex cinema, Arena health and fitness club, shops (e.g. Tesco, Boots and Carpetright) and restaurants (e.g. Harry Ramsden's and Pizza Hut)

- ◆ opened in 1991
- ◆ employs about 350 people in tertiary jobs
- ◆ has 550,000 people living within 15 minutes' drive
- ◆ easily accessible by car, being located at the junction of the Westlink, M2 and M3
- ◆ retained the old red brick factory building, incorporating it into the structure of the new complex
- ◆ has brought the following advantages to people and the economy.

Advantages to people	Advantages to economy
• 350 jobs in service occupations, some full time and some part time so they suit students and mothers of young children, many of whom live nearby • Derelict factory building renovated so that it is no longer an eyesore for local people • Increased choice of shopping and entertainment facilities	• Increased spending in local shops and services as people employed at Yorkgate spend their wages. This brings benefits to the local economy of this inner-city area • With 550,000 people living within easy reach of the complex, the money they spend at Yorkgate allows the new businesses on the site to be profitable

Task 6.2

Three, two, one!

For the Yorkgate case study (or your own case study of change in function of industrial premises) write down:

◆ three facts about the change in function
◆ two advantages to the economy
◆ one fact about the location of the study.

Factors of location of hi-tech industry

You need to:
- *know that economic change has occurred, with the decline of traditional industries and the growth of 'sunrise' industries including hi-tech industry*
- *know the location of hi-tech industry within the British Isles and the factors that explain it.*

Definitions

Industrial location factors are the reasons for industry locating in a particular place.

Technology is the methods or tools which are developed to carry out a task.

Traditional industries were major employers during the nineteenth and early twentieth centuries, e.g. steel, shipbuilding, engineering and textiles.

'Sunrise industries' are rapidly growing and based on high technology and innovation, e.g. mobile phones and games consoles.

Hi-tech industries have developed in the last 20 to 30 years and involve microelectronics, e.g. computers, biotechnology and manufacture of medical equipment.

Infrastructure is the network of services, such as transport links, telephone networks and water supply, which benefit people, industries and businesses.

Traditional industries usually depended on large amounts of coal for power or on imported raw materials, so their location was tied to coalfields or to major ports. Hi-tech industries are not tied like this. The factors affecting their location are transport infrastructure, university links and quality of environment. They tend to cluster together in business parks or science parks that are near to:

◆ motorways and good road links
◆ airports for international links
◆ highly qualified and skilled workers including university graduates
◆ research facilities in universities
◆ pleasant housing and open space
◆ attractive countryside with good leisure facilities.

Silicon chips are used in electronic equipment as semiconductors, so the first concentration of hi-tech industries in California was given the nickname of Silicon Valley. The main concentrations of hi-tech industries in the British Isles are shown in Figure 6.1. They are:

◆ the Central Lowlands of Scotland, between Glasgow and Edinburgh – *Silicon Glen*
◆ the area around Cambridge – *Silicon Fen*
◆ the M4 corridor, from London to Bristol and South Wales – *Silicon Strip*
◆ Technology Parks on the outskirts of Antrim, Galway and Limerick.

Figure 6.1 Location of hi-tech industry in the British Isles

Location factors applied to Antrim Technology Park

Location factors	Statements
Transport infrastructure	• •
University links	•
Quality of environment	• •

Task 6.3

Copy out the table on the previous page, and complete it by selecting appropriate statements from the following list, to illustrate how the location factors apply to Antrim Technology Park.

1 The Park is set in 32 hectares of woodland.
2 Queen's University and the University of Ulster are nearby, at Belfast and Jordanstown.
3 The ports of Larne and Belfast are easily accessible via the M2 motorway.
4 The Giant's Causeway and the Antrim coast provide scenic opportunities for outdoor recreation.
5 Belfast International Airport is only 5 km away.

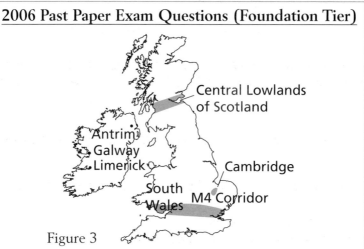

2006 Past Paper Exam Questions (Foundation Tier)

Figure 3

2 **(b)** Study Figure 3 which shows the main areas of hi-tech industries in the British Isles. Answer the questions which follow.

    (i) Name **two** locations in the British Isles which have hi-tech industries. (2)

    (ii) Hi-tech industries require particular factors for their location. Place a ✓ or a ✗ beside each of the statements in the list below to show whether it is or it is not a factor in the location of hi-tech industries in the British Isles. One has been completed for you.

Efficient transport facilities	✓
Lots of workers with low skills	
Bulky raw material	
Near a university or research centre	
Pleasant countryside nearby	(4)

Select your two answers from any of the locations named on the map: Antrim, Galway, Limerick, Central Lowlands of Scotland, South Wales, M4 Corridor or Cambridge.

You know that hi-tech industry has highly skilled workers and uses small, light components such as micro-processors, so 'Lots of workers with low skills' and 'Bulky raw materials' should be marked ✗ and the others ticked as correct.

Unit 2 – The impact of global economic change

Change in the location of manufacturing

You need to:
- *know what a transnational corporation (TNC) is*
- *know the reasons for the shift in location of manufacturing from MEDCs to LEDCs*
- *know the advantages and disadvantages of TNCs for the people and environment of LEDCs*
- *know a global scale case study of a TNC with at least two detailed facts and place names.*

A transnational corporation (also known as a multinational company) operates in many countries, with its headquarters usually in a MEDC and branch factories spread over both LEDCs and MEDCs.

Reasons for the shift in manufacturing location from MEDCs to LEDCs

These may include:

◆ cheaper labour costs in LEDCs (where workers earn a fraction of the average wage of workers in MEDCs)
◆ being nearer to sources of raw materials
◆ access to large markets as LEDC consumers begin to buy more goods
◆ avoiding expensive regulations imposed by MEDC governments concerning health and safety or the environment.

Advantages and disadvantages of TNCs for people and the environment

Advantages	Disadvantages
• Jobs are created, and rates of pay are often higher than the local average • Local people learn new technical skills • **Investment** of large amounts of money into the country's economy • Improved **infrastructure** provided by TNCs such as roads, ports and water supply • Reduced soil erosion as people move away from the countryside to work in urban factories, so there is less overgrazing or over-cultivation	• Only low-skilled work available for local people so wages are low by our standards • Managers from MEDCs often come to do higher paid work • Profits go to the HQ in MEDC rather than being re-invested locally • Decisions made far away in HQ so the TNC may close its LEDC branch suddenly and people will lose their jobs • Powerful TNCs may persuade a LEDC government to have minimal protection for workers • Pollution may occur, e.g. air pollution and dumping of waste products

Task 6.4

Write out the lists of advantages and disadvantages of TNCs, using red for those relating to people, and green for those relating to the environment.

Case study of Nike – a transnational corporation (TNC) at the global scale

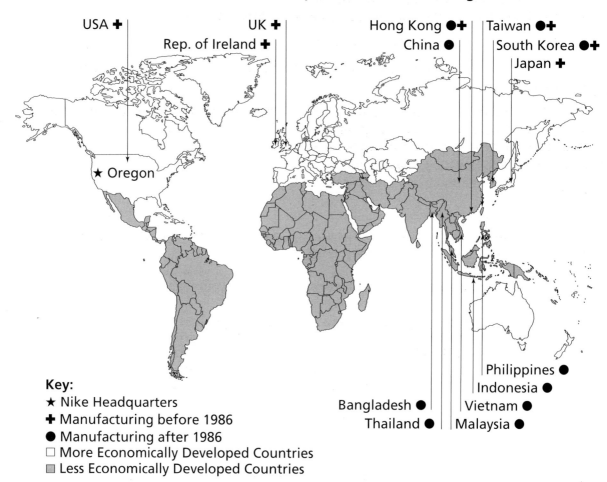

Figure 6.2 Distribution of Nike manufacturing locations around the world

Task 6.5

1 Use Figure 6.2 to find the answers to the following questions.

a Is the headquarters of Nike in a MEDC or a LEDC?
b Was manufacturing before 1986 done in MEDCs, LEDCs or both?
c Is manufacturing today done in MEDCs, LEDCs or both?

2 Memorise the names of:

◆ two MEDCs where Nike goods were made before 1986
◆ two LEDCs where they are made today but weren't made before 1986.

Nike facts:

1 Headquarters in USA does design and marketing
2 Manufacturing is subcontracted to factories in LEDCs
3 Workforce:

◆ around 20,000 people employed directly
◆ around 500,000 people employed by subcontractors in LEDCs

4 Products: sports shoes and other sportswear

The reasons for Nike's change in location of manufacturing, to solely LEDCs, can be summarised as:

◆ Lower labour costs in LEDCs – this allows Nike to keep production costs to a minimum and to maximise profits while competing with Adidas and Reebok
◆ Weaker environmental laws than in MEDCs
◆ Less strict health and safety regulations.

Task 6.6

Study the table of impacts of TNCs on people and the environment (see page 89). Select two advantages and two disadvantages, one each for people and the environment, which you consider may apply to a LEDC, such as Vietnam, where Nike operates.

2006 Past Paper Exam Questions (Higher Tier)

2 (b) (iii) Name **one** transnational corporation (TNC) you have studied and state fully **one** reason why it has changed its location from a MEDC to a LEDC. (4)

You need to name your case study TNC, Nike, and include in your explanation some real facts and locations, e.g. 'Nike moved its production of trainers from USA to Vietnam because Vietnamese workers are paid less than US workers so Nike can make greater profits.'

Unit 3 – Sustainable development strategies

Differences in development between MEDCs and LEDCs

You need to:
- *know the differences between MEDCs and LEDCs*
- *know how we measure development using economic and social indicators.*

MEDCs are More Economically Developed Countries, or richer countries such as the UK or the USA.

LEDCs are Less Economically Developed Countries, or poorer countries such as India or Kenya.

Most MEDCs are in North America and Europe. Most LEDCS are in South America, Africa and Asia. Often a dividing line is drawn on a world map, showing richer countries mostly in the north (but including Australia and New Zealand!) and poorer countries mostly in the south.

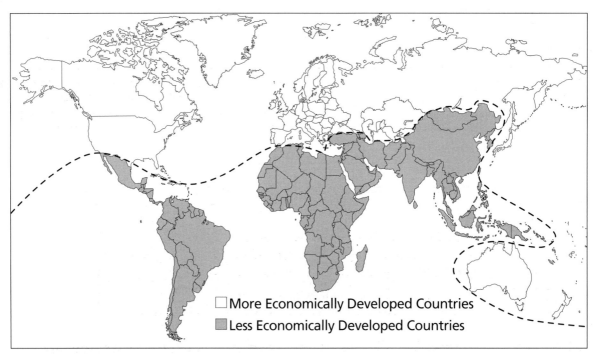

Figure 6.3 North–south divide

Development is difficult to measure. We use lots of different pieces of information to indicate how developed a country is. These are called development indicators. Some are to do with money – these are economic indicators, like how much money is earned. Others are to do with the way people live – these are social indicators, such as the percentage of people who can read and write.

Task 6.7

Copy and complete the table below by filling in the second column.

Social and economic indicators of development

Indicator	Social or economic	MEDCs	LEDCs
1 Gross National Product per person – the value of everything a country produces per person	*economic*	Usually over $5000 per year. USA around $29,000	Usually less than $2000 per year. Some countries under $500
2 Life expectancy – how long people live on average	*social*	Over 75 years	Under 60 years
3 Number of people per doctor	*social*	Not many people per doctor, because there are lots of doctors	Lots of people per doctor because there are very few doctors
4 % who can read and write (literacy rate)	*social*	High	Low
5 % with clean water	*social*	High	Low
6 Exports (goods produced and sold to other countries)	*economic*	82% of world export earnings. Lots of valuable manufactured goods	18% of world export earnings. Mostly cheap primary goods like crops

Appropriate technology and economic development

You need to:
- know what is meant by appropriate technology
- know the positive and negative impacts of appropriate technology
- know one sustainable development project in a LEDC, and its impacts.

Technology is the method or tool which is developed to carry out a task. **Appropriate technology** is technology which is appropriate to the situation. For example, it would be no good giving tractors to farmers in poor countries if they can't get diesel to run them – it wouldn't be **appropriate**. Appropriate technology uses the skills, and suits the needs and level of wealth of local people.

Task 6.8

Copy the table. Tick the options which are most likely to be appropriate for LEDCs.

	Option a	Tick	Option b	Tick
1 Fuel	Uses solar power	✓	Uses coal and oil	
2 Materials	Uses wood from local forests	✓	Uses steel from USA	
3 Maintenance	Local people know how to maintain equipment	✓	Needs lots of experts from Europe	
4 Cost	Costs less than a day's wages	✓	Costs three months' wages	
5 Environmental impact	Causes lots of pollution		Causes very little damage to environment	✓
6 Jobs	Machinery is made in France		Machinery can be made in the village	✓

Appropriate technology is supposed to encourage **sustainable development**. This means improving people's income and standard of living without using up resources, creating pollution or harming people's quality of life. In other words, it has to be sustainable – you must be able to keep it going for a long time without problems.

Case study of sustainable development – kattumarams in India

Fishermen in Tamil Nadu, India, were having problems. The solution was appropriate technology, leading to sustainable development.

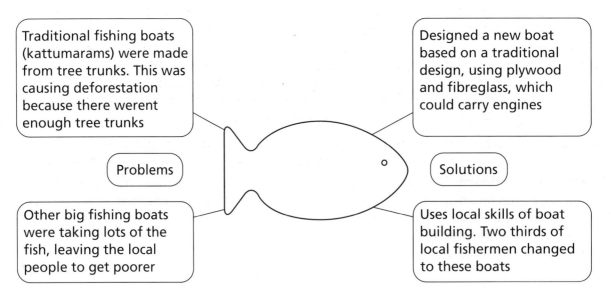

Figure 6.4 Problems and appropriate technology solutions

Impacts

Task 6.9

1 For each of the following impacts, decide whether it is positive or negative.

Fishermen could continue to catch fish and increase their income	Jobs created in boat building
Some materials needed which are not local, e.g. fibreglass	Use of engines contributes to global warming
Can bring more fish to the shore than they could in the old boats	Uses petrol – a scarce resource. This is not sustainable forever

2 Try writing a postcard as if you are one of the fishermen, to your cousin living in Northern Ireland, explaining how your life has changed.

World trade

You need to:
- *know how countries which trade with each other rely on each other*
- *know the problems trade causes*
- *know how Fairtrade can help MEDCs and LEDCs.*

Trade is buying and selling goods and services between one country and another. When a country sells something abroad, it is called an **export**. When a country buys something from another country, it is called an **import**. Countries do this because they cannot all produce everything their people want. This means they rely on each other to get the things they need, and to earn the money to pay for them. This is called **interdependence**. MEDCs and LEDCs need each other. MEDCs depend on LEDCs for food, raw materials and cheap labour. LEDCs depend on MEDCs for investment, expertise and markets.

Some countries earn more money from exports than they spend on imports. This is called a **trade surplus.** Some countries spend more money on imports than they earn from exports. This is called a **trade deficit.**

Task 6.10

Copy the table and fill in the right-hand column, choosing from the terms in bold on page 95. The first one has been done for you.

1	Country A sells steel to other countries	Export
2	Country A buys bananas from other countries	imports
3	Country B only earns £1 million selling bananas, but it needs to spend £3 million buying tractors from abroad	trade deficit
4	Country A earns £5 million from selling steel. It only spends £2 million buying bananas	trade surplus
5	Country B needs to buy tractors for its farmers. It can only afford to buy tractors if it sells enough bananas	interdependence

Globalisation is the way people, goods, money and ideas move round the world faster and more cheaply than ever before. For example, you can get a McDonald's meal or a Coke in most countries in the world, and it will taste almost exactly the same anywhere. Transnational corporations operate all round the world.

Problems of trade

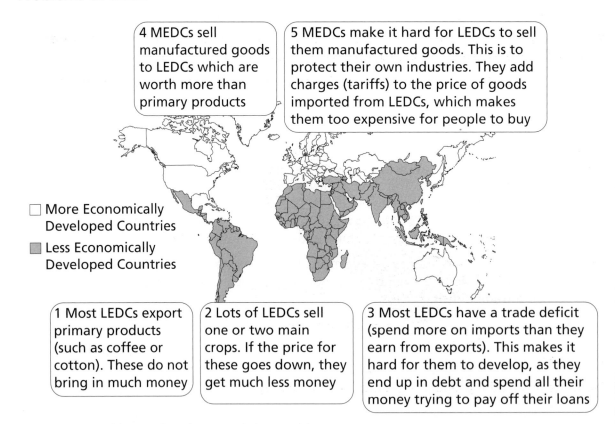

4 MEDCs sell manufactured goods to LEDCs which are worth more than primary products

5 MEDCs make it hard for LEDCs to sell them manufactured goods. This is to protect their own industries. They add charges (tariffs) to the price of goods imported from LEDCs, which makes them too expensive for people to buy

☐ More Economically Developed Countries

☐ Less Economically Developed Countries

1 Most LEDCs export primary products (such as coffee or cotton). These do not bring in much money

2 Lots of LEDCs sell one or two main crops. If the price for these goes down, they get much less money

3 Most LEDCs have a trade deficit (spend more on imports than they earn from exports). This makes it hard for them to develop, as they end up in debt and spend all their money trying to pay off their loans

Figure 6.5 Problems of trade around the world

Task 6.11

1 Copy and complete the following, choosing the correct words.

Most LEDC countries export **raw materials/manufactured goods**. These bring in **lots of/little money**. Most LEDCs depend on **lots of/a few crops**. If prices go down these LEDCs become **richer/poorer**. LEDCs have a trade **deficit/surplus**. They borrow money and this makes it **easier/harder** to develop.

MEDCs sell **raw materials/manufactured goods**. These bring in **lots of/little money**. They try to stop LEDCs selling them goods by adding charges or tariffs which make goods from LEDCs **cheaper/more expensive** for people to buy.

2 As this is quite complicated, try remembering it as two lists of words. Use the lists to make sentences to help you explain the topic to a friend.

LEDCs	MEDCs
Raw materials	Manufactured goods
Little money	Lots of money
Few crops	Tariffs
Prices fall	
Deficit	
Debt	

Fairtrade

Fairtrade means people who make or grow something are paid a fair price for their work. This price is guaranteed, so the producer will not lose out if world prices fall.

If you buy a bar of chocolate which is **not** Fairtrade, the profits are shared as shown in Figure 6.6.

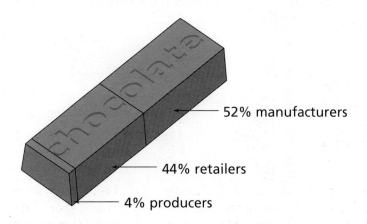

52% manufacturers

44% retailers

4% producers

Figure 6.6

Fairtrade means the producers get more of the money.

Advantages of Fairtrade

For LEDCs	For MEDCs
Guarantees a minimum wage for farmers	Consumers can keep their conscience clear
Farmers can provide for their families	Eventually people in LEDCs will become richer and will be able to buy more imports from MEDCs
Farmers have access to cheap loans	Increases people's understanding of other parts of the world
Farmers control the business	
Profits are used by groups of farmers to help provide health care, education, transport	
Encourages sustainable farming practices	

Task 6.12

Draw a coffee jar or bar of chocolate (or get hold of a real one!) and label it with:

◆ bad things about normal trade in black
◆ good things about Fairtrade in green.

2006 Past Paper Exam Questions

Higher

2 **(d)** Study Figure 5a which shows changes in the market price of coffee. Answer the questions which follow.

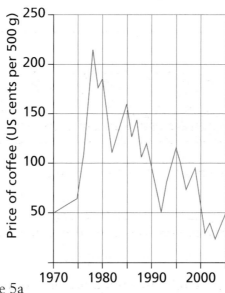

Figure 5a

For full marks you need to refer to the price rising until 1978 and then falling unevenly, as well as quoting figures from the graph, e.g. 'Between 1970 and 1978 the price of coffee rose sharply from 50 cents to 215 cents per 500 g. After 1978 the price fluctuated but fell overall, returning to 50 cents in 2005.'

(i) Describe the changes in the price of coffee on the world market shown in Figure 5a. (3)

Foundation

(e) Study Figure 5b which shows the price paid for coffee on the world market and the price paid by Café Direct (a Fairtrade company) in 2005. Answer the questions which follow.

	World market price (US cents per 500 g of coffee)	Café Direct pays (US cents per 500 g of coffee)
Arabica coffee	120 cents	132 cents

Figure 5b

(i) Explain how Café Direct (the Fairtrade company) helps coffee growers. (3)

(ii) State fully **one** reason why people in MEDCs would want to buy Café Direct coffee rather than cheaper brands of coffee. (3)

(i) This question refers to a table so you should use information from it as well as focusing on how the higher Fairtrade price helps the growers. 'The growers get an extra 12 cents for every 500 g of coffee they sell to Café Direct, so they have more income to spend on educating their children.'

(ii) Think about **one** reason but add elaboration and consequence to gain 3 marks. 'Some people in MEDCs want to buy Café Direct coffee because it makes them feel better to know that coffee growers are being paid fairly and so are able to get better education and health care.'

Aid

You need to:
- *know about different types of aid*
- *know how aid can have positive and negative outcomes.*

Aid is resources given by one country or organisation to another country. These can include:

◆ money (given or loaned)
◆ expertise (people such as engineers, doctors, teachers)
◆ goods – food, technology, equipment such as tents or blankets.

Types of aid
◆ Short-term aid is given when there is an emergency such as a flood.
◆ Long-term aid is given to help a country develop.

Lewis

- ◆ Bilateral aid is when one country gives aid directly to another.
- ◆ Multilateral aid is when lots of governments give money to world organisations such as the UN, who then give it to countries that need it.
- ◆ Tied aid is when the country giving the money tells a country what to spend it on.
- ◆ Voluntary Organisations are charities such as Comic Relief or Oxfam. They get their money from people rather than governments.

Task 6.13

Decide what type of aid is happening in each of the following examples. Some may be more than one type.

1 Many people contribute to a fund to help people after the Boxing Day Tsunami (2 types).
2 Ireland gives money to Mozambique (1 type).
3 Wealthy countries pay money into the World Bank, and it gives loans to poorer countries for irrigation projects (2 types).
4 Granny gets sponsored to abseil down the Europa hotel wearing a chicken costume to raise money for Comic Relief, who will send it to a village in Africa where they want to finish building a school (2 types).

Positive and negative outcomes of aid

Task 6.14

Below are possible outcomes of aid. Decide whether each is positive or negative.

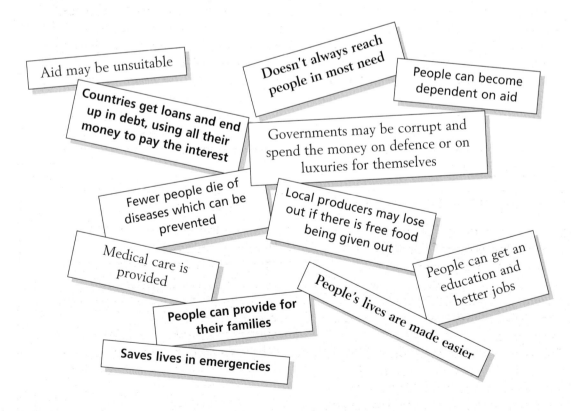

Figure 6.7 Possible outcomes of aid

KNOWLEDGE TESTS

Knowledge Test I (Pages 84–88)

1 What is secondary economic activity?
2 For the case study of change in function of industrial premises, describe the location of the Yorkgate site.
3 What was the site's original use?
4 What is the site's new use?
5 How many tertiary jobs were created?
6 What is infrastructure?
7 What type of transport links influence the location of hi-tech industry?
8 What type of workforce is required by hi-tech industry?
9 Name the three 'silicon' locations of hi-tech industries in the British Isles.
10 Name a Technology Park in Ireland.

KNOWLEDGE TESTS

Knowledge Test II (Pages 89–91)

1 What do the letters TNC stand for?
2 Why might a TNC prefer to employ workers in a LEDC?
3 What kind of regulations do MEDC governments impose on TNCs if they manufacture there?
4 Are the headquarters of a TNC usually in a MEDC or a LEDC?
5 Where do the profits that a TNC makes in LEDCs go?
6 State one advantage of TNCs for people in a LEDC.
7 State one disadvantage of TNCs for the environment in a LEDC.
8 Name one MEDC where Nike goods were manufactured before 1986.
9 Name one LEDC where Nike goods are manufactured today.
10 Approximately how many workers are employed (a) directly by Nike, (b) by subcontractors making Nike goods?

KNOWLEDGE TESTS

Knowledge Test III (Pages 92–100)

1 Are the following indicators of development economic or social? (a) literacy rate, (b) life expectancy, (c) Gross National Product
2 Which countries, MEDCs or LEDCs, generally export primary products such as food crops?
3 What is appropriate technology?
4 What is sustainable development?
5 State two positive impacts of the new boats used by fishermen in Tamil Nadu, India?
6 What are the new boats called?
7 What is a trade deficit?
8 Why does a trade deficit make it harder for a LEDC to develop?
9 How might a farmer's family benefit from Fairtrade?
10 What type of aid is given by many people to help those suffering as a result of an earthquake or famine?

Chapter 7

THEME F:
SETTLEMENTS AND
CHANGE

Unit 1 – Settlement development

Physical and economic site factors

You need to:
- *know that the original site of a settlement reflected the needs of the people who set it up*
- *know examples of physical and economic factors affecting the site and subsequent growth of settlements*
- *know how to describe the site of a settlement from evidence on OS maps, sketch maps and photographs.*

A **settlement** is a place where people live. Settlements range in size from single farmhouses and small hamlets (groups of houses) to villages, towns and cities. The **site** of the settlement is the actual spot where it is built, whereas the **location** describes where it is in relation to its surroundings (other settlements, rivers, mountains and roads). The **distribution** of settlements refers to how they are spread out: they may be widely dispersed in an upland area with few resources, or clustered along a river valley or coastline.

The original settlers needed food, water and shelter. They therefore selected a site near a stream or spring for drinking water, with land nearby that was suitable for grazing or for growing crops and with supplies of timber for building and for firewood.

A **wet point site** has water supply as its most important factor. In chalk and limestone areas, where most water flows underground, spring-line settlements grew up where springs emerged from the ground. People who feared attack selected a **defensive site**. They would choose a site on a hilltop or one surrounded by the meander bend of a river, as these would be easier to defend.

A **bridging point** is a site where a river could be crossed most easily, and as it became the focus where tracks and roads converged, the settlement that grew up there often became a successful market town.

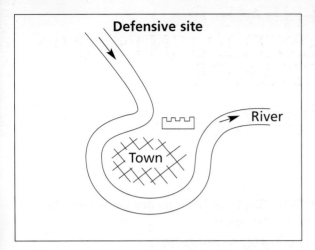

Defensive site

Defensive site protected on three sides by the river and by the castle on the fourth side

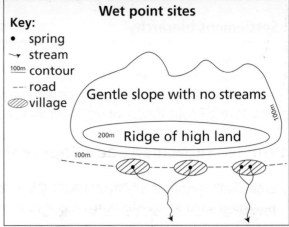

Wet point sites

Key:
- spring
- stream
- 100m contour
- road
- village

Gentle slope with no streams

200m Ridge of high land

100m

100m

Spring-line villages occupy wet point sites

Figure 7.1

While shelter, water supply and defence are physical site factors there are also economic site factors such as transport communications, which serve to make settlements more accessible, and resources such as farmland, timber and minerals. Evidence can often be found by studying an Ordnance Survey map or sketch map. The OS map found in *Geography for CCEA GCSE* (page 44) shows the site of the village of Cushendun in grid square 2432. This site has:

◆ shelter from prevailing SW winds by surrounding hills over 300 metres, e.g. Gruig Top (GR 2030)
◆ a bridging point, where the B92 crosses the Glendun River
◆ an area of flat land nearby (the Glendun floodplain) suitable for farming, in contrast to the very steep slopes of the valley sides.

Task 7.1

Study the OS map of Carnlough found in *Geography for CCEA GCSE* page 177. Describe the site of Carnlough by considering the following points:

a height of the land Carnlough is built on
b aspect (direction the slope is facing)
c shelter, if any
d water supply
e natural harbour.

Where possible, quote the grid reference and/or name of the map features you mention, as this shows that you have found them on the map and not just guessed.

Settlement hierarchy

> *You need to:*
> - *know what is meant by hierarchy*
> - *know that settlements can be arranged in a hierarchy according to their size and function.*

A **settlement hierarchy** is an arrangement of settlements in order of their size and importance. In a region there may be only one large city, several smaller towns, dozens of villages and hundreds of farmhouses. The numerous small settlements are close together but large settlements, which are few in number, are far apart.

The **sphere of influence** of a settlement is its market area, that is the area from which people travel to use its services. The **range** is the maximum distance that people travel to obtain a service and the **threshold** is the minimum number of people needed to ensure that a service will be able to stay in business. This means that a city at the top of the settlement hierarchy has a large sphere of influence attracting people from nearby towns and villages to use its wide variety of services, many of which have a large range and threshold. A village, near the bottom of the settlement hierarchy, has a small sphere of influence as it only serves its own population and the surrounding farmhouses. The services it offers are limited to those such as a village shop and primary school, which only need a small threshold population to survive.

Figure 7.2 Settlement hierarchy

The **function** of a settlement is its main economic activity, for example port, market town, mining town or tourist resort. Large settlements near the top of a hierarchy will have more functions than small settlements near the bottom. People who live in farmhouses and hamlets will need to visit their nearest village to find a shop or primary school, while people from towns and villages will have to go to a city to find a university, museum or major concert venue.

Task 7.2

Study Figure 7.3 showing the settlement pattern in Coquetdale, Northumberland. Write out and complete the paragraph that follows, selecting words and numbers from the list provided.

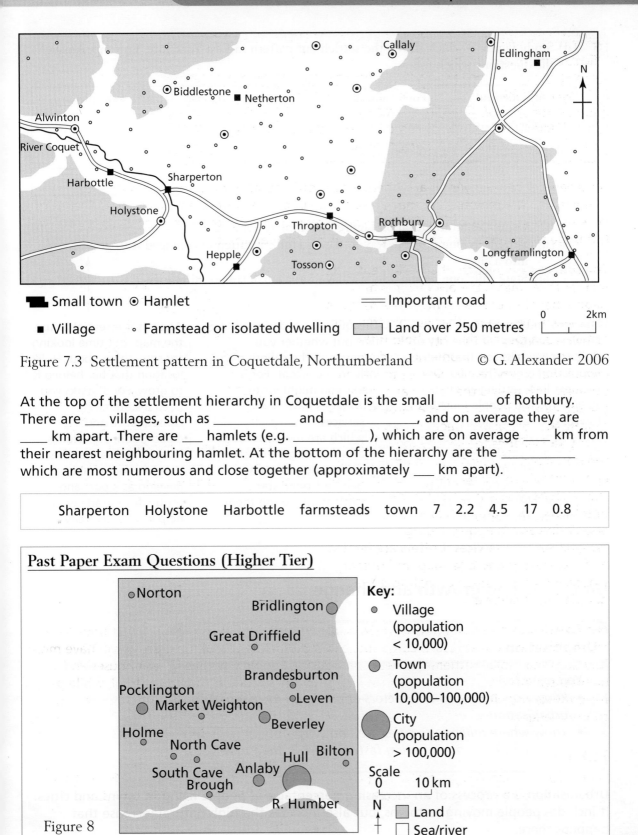

Small town ⊙ Hamlet   ═══ Important road

■ Village   ◦ Farmstead or isolated dwelling   Land over 250 metres   0   2km

Figure 7.3 Settlement pattern in Coquetdale, Northumberland   © G. Alexander 2006

At the top of the settlement hierarchy in Coquetdale is the small _____ of Rothbury. There are ___ villages, such as _____ and _____, and on average they are ____ km apart. There are ___ hamlets (e.g. _____), which are on average ____ km from their nearest neighbouring hamlet. At the bottom of the hierarchy are the _____ which are most numerous and close together (approximately ___ km apart).

Sharperton   Holystone   Harbottle   farmsteads   town   7   2.2   4.5   17   0.8

Past Paper Exam Questions (Higher Tier)

Figure 8

3 **(d)** Study Figure 8 which shows the settlement pattern in East Yorkshire, England. Answer the questions which follow.

Type of settlement	Population size	Total number on map	Example
City		1	Hull
	10, 000–100, 000		
		10	Holme

Table 2

    (i)   Using the information on Figure 8, complete Table 2. (6)

    (ii) State fully **one** possible way in which Hull's location encouraged it to grow into a city. (3)

    (iii) State fully **one** reason why a village has a small sphere of influence. (3)

The map and key provide all the answers. Starting with the city of Hull, the key tells you that Hull's population is over 100,000. On the next line, settlements with 10,000–100,000 people must be towns. You can see four settlements with this symbol on the map and you have the choice of Bridlington, Pocklington, Beverley or Anlaby as an example. Finally, there are ten villages, such as Holme, with fewer than 10,000 people.

This question is designed to find out whether you understand the sphere of influence concept. For 3 marks you might write:
- 'Villages have few services
- which are low order such as a pub or general store
- so they do not attract people from distant settlements to use them.'

Again it is essential to use the map, this time looking for something about Hull's location that has helped it to grow. For 3 marks you need a statement, consequence and •elaboration• e.g. 'Hull is located beside the River Humber, so it could develop as a port and •profits from trade would help it grow as a city.•

Unit 2 – Urban growth and change

Urbanisation

You need to:
- *know how push and pull factors and natural increase cause urbanisation*
- *know where millionaire cities are and why*
- *know why cities are growing faster in LEDCs than in MEDCs.*

Urbanisation is a process of an increasing percentage of people living in towns and cities. It includes people moving to towns, but also includes the high natural increase that happens there.

Causes of urbanisation

High natural increase in cities – more people being born than dying. This is because:

◆ lots of young people migrate to the city, then want to start a family
◆ more babies are born alive in towns because of better health care

◆ death rate is lower because there are lots of young people and better health care.

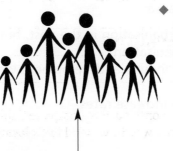

Push factors push people away from the countryside

Pull factors pull people towards the cities

Figure 7.4 Causes of urbanisation

Task 7.3

Decide whether each of the following is a push factor or a pull factor.

a Lack of job opportunities
b Good health care
c Natural disaster
d Good education
e Good public services, such as piped water

Millionaire cities

Millionaire cities are cities with more than 1 million people living in them. In 1950 most of these were in MEDCs. The biggest was New York in the USA with 12 million people. By 2000 most of these were in LEDCs. The biggest was Mexico City in Mexico with 25 million people.

This change has happened because:

◆ MEDCs experienced lots of urbanisation in the past, but lots of people now want to move away from cities (counterurbanisation).
◆ LEDCs are now getting more industrial development which attracts people to move to the city.
◆ LEDCs also have high natural increase rates.

Rates of city growth

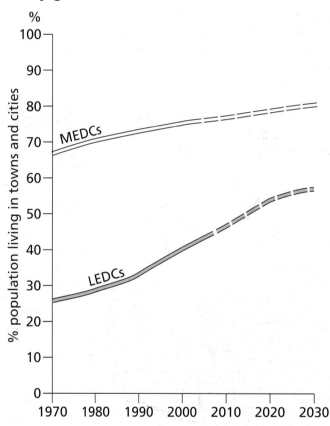

Figure 7.5 Graph comparing urbanisation in MEDCs and LEDCs. Reproduced with the permission of Nelson Thornes Ltd.

Task 7.4

1 What percentage of people in MEDCs lived in urban areas in 1980?
2 What percentage of people in MEDCs lived in urban areas in 2000?
3 What percentage of people in LEDCs lived in urban areas in 1980?
4 What percentage of people in LEDCs lived in urban areas in 2000?
5 Was the biggest change in MEDCs or LEDCs?

The reasons for these changes in growth are the same as the reasons for the location of millionaire cities.

Locations of land use zones in cities

You need to:
- *know what the different zones in cities are*
- *know where you find each zone in MEDCs and LEDCs*
- *know one city in a MEDC.*

Land use means what the land is used for, for example shops, industry, housing.

Land use zones, or **functional zones**, are areas which have mainly one land use. Housing or residential areas can be divided into **socio-economic areas**. These are areas which have different levels of wealth. Cities often also have **ethnic areas**, where members of specific ethnic groups tend to live close together.

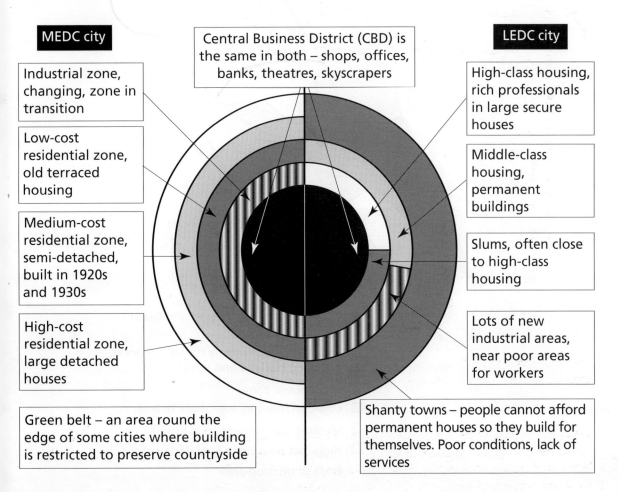

MEDC city

Industrial zone, changing, zone in transition

Low-cost residential zone, old terraced housing

Medium-cost residential zone, semi-detached, built in 1920s and 1930s

High-cost residential zone, large detached houses

Green belt – an area round the edge of some cities where building is restricted to preserve countryside

Central Business District (CBD) is the same in both – shops, offices, banks, theatres, skyscrapers

LEDC city

High-class housing, rich professionals in large secure houses

Middle-class housing, permanent buildings

Slums, often close to high-class housing

Lots of new industrial areas, near poor areas for workers

Shanty towns – people cannot afford permanent houses so they build for themselves. Poor conditions, lack of services

Figure 7.6 Land use zones in cities in MEDCs and LEDCs

Task 7.5

Using Figure 7.6, decide whether each of the following statements is likely to apply to cities in MEDCs or LEDCs, or both.

a Residential zones become wealthier as you go out from the city centre to the edge of the city.
b The wealthiest areas of housing are likely to be near the city centre.
c Most of the shops and offices are in the city centre.
d Mr and Mrs Da Silva migrated from a village and built their own house on the edge of the city.
e Mr and Mrs Jones are retired and live in a large four-bedroom detached house on the edge of the city.
f David looks out of the window of his large house, and sees a security guard and an old slum building across the road.

Case study of one city in a MEDC – Belfast

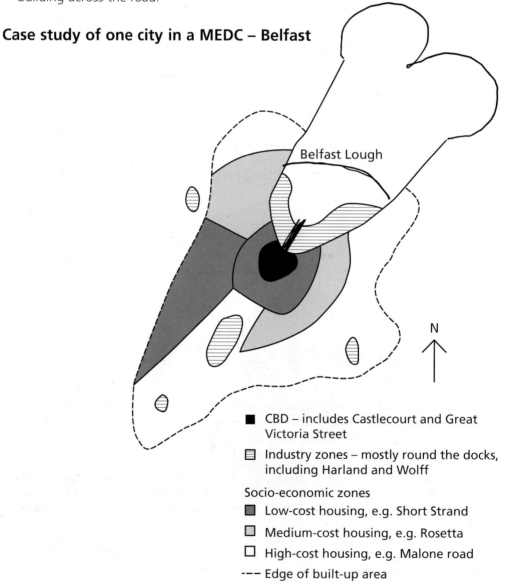

Figure 7.7 Land use zones in Belfast

■ CBD – includes Castlecourt and Great Victoria Street

▤ Industry zones – mostly round the docks, including Harland and Wolff

Socio-economic zones

▨ Low-cost housing, e.g. Short Strand

▨ Medium-cost housing, e.g. Rosetta

☐ High-cost housing, e.g. Malone road

--- Edge of built-up area

Change in urban areas

You need to:
- *know what has changed in urban areas*
- *know why these changes happen*
- *know what positive and negative impacts these changes have on people and on the environment*
- *know what the management response has been*
- *know changes in your case study city.*

Change	Causes	Impacts	Management response	Change in Belfast
Housing – old terraced houses replaced with high-rise blocks of flats in 1960s	Old housing was run down, overcrowded, lacked water, electricity and heating	Better facilities provided and loss of old communities. Flats were dangerous, unsightly, badly designed	Eventually many of these have been demolished and replaced with low-rise housing	Areas of West Belfast, e.g. Divis flats
Old terraced houses now being renewed – kept and improved	As above	Better facilities, people have stayed in local communities		Inner city areas, e.g. Lower Newtownards Road
Industries leaving inner cities	Crowded areas, no room for expansion, narrow congested roads, cheaper to move to outskirts or abroad	Loss of jobs. Land and buildings left derelict	Money has been made available for redevelopment, e.g. Laganside, Odyssey	Docks area along M2 and near River Lagan
Shops – small corner shops closed, large supermarkets opened on edge of city (the **urban fringe**)	More people using cars, people have fridges and freezers so they don't have to shop every day	Elderly and people without cars are left with fewer local shops. More car use causes pollution. Convenient for many shoppers		Out-of-town shopping areas – Forestside, Knocknagoney, Abbey Centre
Counterurbanisation – people moving out of cities and towns to rural areas	Want to get away from noise, crowding, pollution	City areas lose population, therefore schools, shops, doctors' surgeries and other services may close	Limit planning permission for new houses in the countryside	Belfast population decreased as people moved to Lisburn, Bangor, Newtownards, Holywood

…sk 7.6

Make a spider diagram to show changes in urban areas, based on the outline below. Use different colours to show the changes, the causes, impacts, management responses and information about your case study.

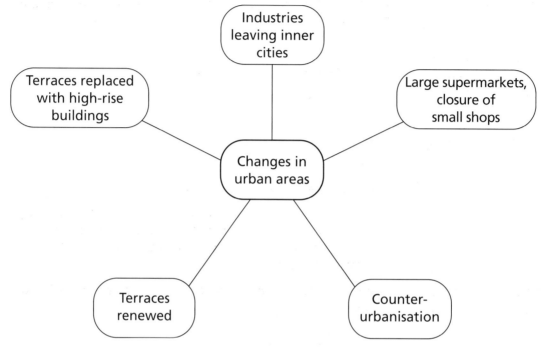

Figure 7.8

Unit 3 – Planning sustainability for urban environments

Improving and regenerating inner cities

You need to:
- know what has been done to improve:
  - *built environments*
  - *green spaces*
  - *amenities*
  - *housing*
  - *employment*
  - *waste management*
- *be able to evaluate whether these have been good or bad for the local community*
- *be able to give this information for your case study of an urban planning initiative.*

Planning for sustainability

Planning is a process where decisions are made about how land should be used, what transport and other facilities are needed, and what should be protected.

Sustainable development of cities means that they should grow in a way that meets our needs today without making it difficult for future generations to meet their own needs.

Sustainable cities should:

◆ provide enough jobs
◆ provide housing at prices to suit different people
◆ reduce, reuse, recycle
◆ have health care available
◆ provide education for all
◆ keep historical buildings (**conservation**)
◆ use mostly public transport, and have little congestion.

Case study of an urban planning initiative – Laganside

The inner area of Belfast, around the docks, became very run down, because industries were moving out and people moved out. The River Lagan at low tide had large areas of mud which were smelly and ugly. The Laganside Corporation was set up in the 1990s with the job of regenerating the area along the Lagan.

Regeneration means taking action to try to give an area new life – improving the buildings, bringing in new employment, providing social facilities etc.

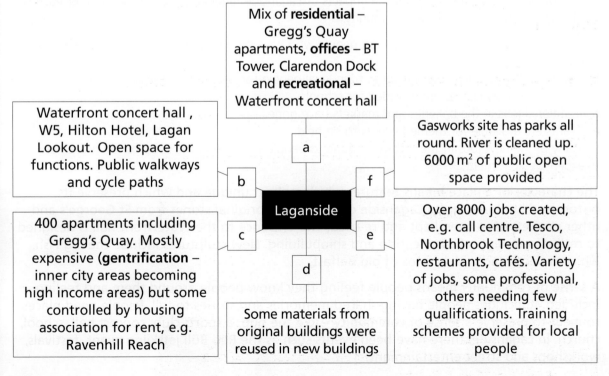

Mix of **residential** – Gregg's Quay apartments, **offices** – BT Tower, Clarendon Dock and **recreational** – Waterfront concert hall

Waterfront concert hall, W5, Hilton Hotel, Lagan Lookout. Open space for functions. Public walkways and cycle paths

Gasworks site has parks all round. River is cleaned up. 6000 m² of public open space provided

b | **Laganside** | **f**
a
c | **e**
d

400 apartments including Gregg's Quay. Mostly expensive (**gentrification** – inner city areas becoming high income areas) but some controlled by housing association for rent, e.g. Ravenhill Reach

Some materials from original buildings were reused in new buildings

Over 8000 jobs created, e.g. call centre, Tesco, Northbrook Technology, restaurants, cafés. Variety of jobs, some professional, others needing few qualifications. Training schemes provided for local people

Figure 7.9

113

Task 7.7

Replace the letters a–f with the correct headings, choosing from the list below:

◆ Housing
◆ Employment
◆ Built environment
◆ Green spaces
◆ Waste management
◆ Amenities

Evaluation – problems and benefits for the local communities

You need to:
- *be able to evaluate the impacts of regeneration measures (both positive and negative)*
- *be able to identify efforts which have been made to conserve character and a sense of community*
- *give this information for your case study of an urban planning initiative.*

Task 7.8

The following are statements about the impacts of Laganside regeneration. Decide whether each is positive or negative for the local community.

a House prices have gone up and young people who have grown up in the area cannot afford to buy houses.
b Training schemes have been set up to train local people for new jobs in the area.
c Free water-safety classes are provided for schools.
d Traditional jobs in the bakeries and markets have gone.
e Grants are available for themed events to be held.
f Many of the new jobs in the area have gone to people who live in the suburbs, or in the new expensive apartments.

The character of a place means features which make it unique and which preserve its history and heritage. In the Laganside development, original stones from St George's and other markets have been kept and re-used. The entrance to the Waterfront hall is designed to reflect aeronautical engineering and shipbuilding. New sculptures include the Big Fish, which is decorated with photos of old Belfast.

A sense of community means people feeling they know people around them and feeling included. It includes people having shared memories and stories to tell. People need places to meet to preserve a sense of community – like the pub, a sports club, concert hall, school, church. In Laganside, there have been events such as the Red Bull jetskiing event, festivals, workshops and street entertainment.

2006 Past Paper Exam Questions (Foundation Tier)

3 (e) For a named inner city regeneration scheme you have studied, state fully how the housing and employment opportunities have been improved. (7)

There is one mark for correctly naming a suitable inner city scheme (e.g. Laganside, Belfast) and 3 marks each for answers under the headings of improvement to housing and improvement to employment opportunities. As this is a case study answer you need to include facts such as figures and place names. For housing you could write 'Derelict housing has been demolished and new apartments built, e.g. at Gregg's Quay.' For employment, 'About 8000 jobs have been created including hi-tech jobs at Northbrook Technology.'

Waste management

Waste management is how litter and other waste is dealt with. For a long time, waste in Northern Ireland has mostly gone to landfill sites, where it is simply buried underground. This is unsustainable, as it causes pollution and we will run out of suitable sites for landfill.

By 2020 the UK aims to have less than a third of its waste going to landfill. The Wake up to Waste campaign aims to encourage people to reduce, reuse and recycle. Many areas now have kerbside collection for recycling plastic, paper, cans and compostable garden waste. Some are suggesting weighing bins and charging people based on the amount of waste produced. It now costs more to use landfill because the government charges more tax for it.

Task 7.9

Put the following waste management options in order from most to least sustainable.

incineration (burning waste)   recycling   reuse   composting   landfill   reducing

Measures to control traffic

You need to:
- *know what has been done to control traffic in one city in the EU (not the British Isles)*
- *know how this ensures the sustainable development of the city.*

Problems of traffic:

◆ congestion
◆ danger to cyclists and pedestrians
◆ pollution.

Case study – Freiburg, Germany

The city – 200,000 people, Southern Germany, old walled city centre

Problems – population growth in 1980s, increased traffic congestion

FREIBURG – solutions to traffic problems

Solutions

◆ Pedestrian zones in city centre
◆ Improved public transport, very cheap fares
◆ Integration between public transport services
◆ 200 miles of cycle paths, repair facilities, showers at station
◆ No free parking
◆ City is compact, less travelling is needed

Impacts

◆ 4000 fewer cars each day than in 1970
◆ Only 40% of trips made by car
◆ Public transport use more than doubled since 1980
◆ All this reduces congestion, fuel use and pollution, ensuring that Freiburg's development is sustainable.

Figure 7.10

Task 7.10

One, two, three!
State:

◆ one problem Freiburg was experiencing
◆ two solutions it adopted
◆ three pieces of evidence that it is ensuring Freiburg's development is sustainable.

KNOWLEDGE TESTS

Knowledge Test I (Pages 102–106)

1 What is the name for the actual spot on which a settlement is built?
2 Where might a settlement be built in order to make it easy to defend?
3 Why is a settlement at a bridging point likely to grow?
4 What is settlement hierarchy?
5 Does a village or a city have a larger sphere of influence?
6 True or false? Small settlements are closer together than larger ones.
7 True or false? There are more large settlements than small ones.
8 What term means the maximum distance that people travel to obtain a service?
9 Name a service, with a small range and threshold, which may be found in villages as well as towns or cities.
10 What function might a settlement have because it is situated at the coast?

KNOWLEDGE TESTS

Knowledge Test II (Pages 106–112)

1 If a farm worker moves to a city because machinery is increasingly used on farms instead of manpower, is this a push or a pull factor?
2 True or false? A millionaire city is a city with more than a million people living in it.
3 True or false? Today most millionaire cities are located in MEDCs.
4 Many people are moving out of cities in MEDCs. What is this process called?
5 What is the name for an area around the edge of some cities where building is restricted in order to preserve the countryside?
6 In a LEDC city, are shanty towns found close to the CBD or on the edge of the city?
7 In Belfast, what replaced the old terraced houses in the 1960s?
8 Why did the terraced houses need to be replaced?
9 What has been one impact in Belfast of industries moving away from inner city locations?
10 What is one impact in Belfast of the growth of out-of-town shopping centres?

KNOWLEDGE TESTS

Knowledge Test III (Pages 112–116)

1 State one example of how the Laganside planning initiative has improved green spaces in the area.
2 Name two public amenities provided as part of the Laganside planning initiative.
3 Name a housing area built as part of the Laganside planning initiative.
4 Approximately how many jobs have been created in Laganside?
5 What is being done to encourage better waste management in Belfast?
6 Why did traffic congestion increase in Freiburg, southern Germany, in the 1980s?
7 How is cycling encouraged in Freiburg?
8 How is the use of public transport encouraged in Freiburg?
9 How is commuting by car discouraged in Freiburg?
10 How has Freiburg's car use changed since 1970 as a result of these policies?

Chapter 8

ANSWERS TO KNOWLEDGE TESTS AND TASKS

Chapter 2

KNOWLEDGE TEST I

1 (a) Anemometer, (b) Rain gauge
2 (a) Millibars (mb), (b) °C
3 Polar maritime, cold and wet
4 (a) High, (b) Sinking
5 (b) Warm and cold fronts
6 Depression
7 Anticyclone
8 Depression
9 Cold front
10 Two of farmers, builders, retailers or similar

KNOWLEDGE TEST II

1 (a) False, (b) True
2 Winter
3 15° C, 4 °C, 650 mm
4 Any two of wheat, barley, potatoes
5 Crops ripen quickly
6 Irrigation of crops during drought or heaters/polythene covers to protect from frost
7 25 °C, 10 °C, 450 mm
8 Two of olives, grapes oranges, lemons, peaches, vegetables
9 Drought in summer **or** frost damage to vines **or** poor olive and grape quality if too much winter rain
10 Irrigation of citrus, rice and cotton crops **or** polythene tunnels for vegetable production

KNOWLEDGE TEST III

1 Carbon dioxide
2 Increasing car ownership, as population and standard of living increase
3 Low-lying coasts and high population density
4 Increased risk of hurricane damage and loss of life
5 Increased income from tourism (e.g. Brighton) and new crops (e.g. vines and sunflowers)
6 Extinction
7 Three of solar, wave, wind power, tidal, geothermal, HEP.
8 Afforestation
9 People may buy more fuel-efficient cars or use public transport
10 The World Summit for Sustainable Development

TASK 2.1 (page 8)

Pressure: barometer, millibars (mb)
Temperature: max/min thermometer, °C
Precipitation: rain gauge, mm

Wind speed: anemometer, kph
Wind direction: wind vane, 8 points of the compass

TASK 2.2 (page 8)

1 cold, moist
2 cold, dry
3 warm, dry
4 warm, moist

TASK 2.3 (page 10)

1 D   2 SA   3 D   4 WA   5 D   6 WA   7 D   8 SA   9 SA

TASK 2.4 (page 10)

1 B   2 E   3 D   4 C   5 A   6 F

TASK 2.5 (page 11)

Motorists – any two of icy roads, fog, flooded roads, fallen trees in a storm. Sailors – gale or storm force winds, fog. Knowing about the weather conditions in advance means drivers can avoid certain roads, or sailors can delay journeys.

TASK 2.6 (page 15)

2 Latitude: Rome is closer to the equator, where the sun's rays heat the earth more intensely
3 Prevailing winds: Ireland is next to the Atlantic, so winds from SW carry lots of moisture to Ireland. Winds reaching Moscow have been blowing over land and are dry.
4 Continentality: The sea is warmer than land in the winter, so the sea keeps Ireland warm. It is cooler than land in summer, so it keeps Ireland cool.

Chapter 3

KNOWLEDGE TEST I

1 Convection currents in the mantle
2 Pacific Ocean
3 Constructive
4 Destructive
5 San Andreas fault on the boundary of the Pacific and North American plates
6 Focus
7 Eurasian, Pacific and Philippine plates
8 (a) 5,500 people dead, (b) $\frac{1}{4}$ million homeless
9 Broken gas mains caused fires
10 MEDCs have better equipped and trained emergency teams **or** better designed buildings and bridges **or** better transport networks so help arrives faster

KNOWLEDGE TEST II

1 Tributary
2 They get smaller and more rounded as they knock against each other and the river banks
3 The amount of water passing a point in a certain time
4 True
5 False
6 Inside of a bend where water is shallower and slower so deposition occurs
7 Alluvium/sediment/the river's load
8 Urbanisation **or** narrowing a river channel **or** draining wetlands **or** deforestation
9 Soft engineering
10 Wildlife is encouraged such as the beaver and bald eagle

KNOWLEDGE TEST III

1 Sedimentary
2 Bedding planes
3 Chemical weathering
4 Swallow hole, limestone pavement
5 Up from the floor of the cave
6 £56 million
7 Spring gentian
8 Quarrying is banned by law
9 18%
10 Government pays subsidies to farmers whose animals continue to graze the hills

TASK 3.2 (page 26)

1 oceanic plate
2 ocean trench
3 earthquake focus
4 volcano

5 continental plate
6 mantle

Both arrowheads should point towards centre of diagram.

TASK 3.4 (page 29)

a source
b mouth, estuary
c watershed

d tributary
e drainage basin

TASK 3.5 (page 30)

Near source: narrow, shallow, low discharge, large and angular load

Near mouth: wide, deep, high discharge, small and rounded load

TASK 3.6 (page 32)

a Erosion
b Transportation, suspension
c Erosion

d Deposition
e Transportation, traction or saltation

TASK 3.7 (page 33)

Inside: slower flow, less energy, deposition, slip-off slope, shallow water

Outside: faster flow, lots of energy, erosion, river cliff, deep water

TASK 3.8 (page 34)

a Bluff
b Floodplain

c River channel
d Deposition

TASK 3.9 (page 35)

1 (b) deforestation, less water used up by plants, H
  (c) saturates the ground, P

  (d) glacier or snow melting, P
  (e) urbanisation, H
2 +, –, –, +, –, –, +, –, –, +, –

TASK 3.10 (page 36)

Soft, hard, hard, soft, soft, hard

TASK 3.12 (page 42)

Limestone, bedding planes, joints, water, carbonic acid, calcium carbonate, dissolves

TASK 3.13 (page 43)

a limestone pavement
b cave
c stalagmite

d stalactite
e swallow hole

Chapter 4

KNOWLEDGE TEST I

1 See Glossary
2 Taiga
3 Grasses, some trees, zebra, lions etc.
4 800 mm, 16 °C
5 Ash, oak, bluebell, Forest Bug
6 1800 mm, over 25 °C

7 Two of mahogany, ebony, rosewood
8 Nutrients leached out of soil, soil washed away
9 Producers
10 Food web is more complex than a food chain, with many interdependent plants and animals

KNOWLEDGE TEST II

1 Three of draining, peat extraction, grazing, afforestation
2 Sphagnum moss, sundew
3 14 km
4 Peat is compacted, soil is left bare and becomes eroded
5 Site of Special Scientific Interest, Environmentally Sensitive Area
6 Slash and burn

7 Advance Brazil
8 Animals lose their habitat and food supply. So much forest is cleared that they cannot all find homes and food in the forest that remains.
9 10%
10 Local people can continue to live and work in the area and develop sustainable economic activities, e.g. using fruit and rubber trees

KNOWLEDGE TEST III

1 See Glossary
2 In western Kenya, 150 km from Nairobi
3 Tents or stone-built lodges
4 Game wardens, guides, drivers, cooks, cleaners
5 Seasonal work leaves some people unemployed for part of the year

6 Profits used to fund schools, health and community projects
7 Grass is destroyed if vehicles leave the tracks, and soil is eroded
8 25 metres

TASK 4.2 (page 49)

	Climate	Soil	Vegetation
Climate		Temperatures above 25 °C and 1800 mm rain per year (heavy rain every afternoon) mean dead leaves etc decompose very quickly, and rock underneath the soil weather quickly. Heavy rain may leach lots of nutrients away and wash soil away if there are no trees to protect it.	High rainfall and temperatures mean lots of plants eg. mahogany and ebony trees, can grow (high biodiversity) and get very tall, about 40 m. Lots of rain means trees have waxy leaves so water runs off instead of making them rot.
Soil			Soil is deep but not very fertile as most nutrients get leached away by heavy rain. Most plants have shallow roots to get nutrients from the top layer of soil.
Vegetation	Tall trees provide lots of shade, so not many plants grow on the ground. Some ferns grow here. Most other plants grow in clearings.	There are always lots of dead leaves falling, providing nutrients to the soil. The plants hold the soil together and stop it washing away.	

TASK 4.3 (page 51)

1 Fig 4.4 oak trees and snowberry bushes = producers, all others = consumers
Fig 4.5 mahogany and ebony trees = producers, all others = consumers

2 There are lots of possibilities:
oak trees – red squirrel – long eared owl
snowberry bushes – fieldmouse – badger
trees – butterflies – lizards – anaconda
trees – spider monkey – people

TASK 4.5 (page 54)

Local communities, vegetation/animals, animals, soil/vegetation, soil/vegetation, local communities

Chapter 5

KNOWLEDGE TEST I

1 Bangladesh, W. Europe
2 Deep rich soils are deposited by rivers
3 Subsistence rice farming
4 40 million approx., 75%
5 The Meseta (central plain)
6 Continentality (distance from the sea)
7 Pyrenees
8 Mediterranean climate (hot, dry sunny summers) attracts tourists so there are many jobs in tourism
9 Madrid, 3 million
10 Barcelona, Bilbao

KNOWLEDGE TEST II

1 Grow rapidly
2 Decrease
3 Lower birth rate
4 Lower birth rate as more children survive
5 Mexico
6 (a) 0–14, (b) 65+
7 Youth dependent

8 A person who moves out of a country permanently
9 Migrants may do unpleasant jobs for low wages or bring valuable skills to the workforce
10 One of racial intolerance and discrimination, language difficulties, residential segregation

KNOWLEDGE TEST III

1 Resources
2 At an adequate standard of living
3 Lack of resources or depletion (using up) of resources
4 Overgrazing, leading to soil erosion and famine
5 Coal, oil and natural gas
6 Three of wind power, wave, tidal, geothermal, solar and HEP

7 Lendrum's Bridge, Co Tyrone or Corkey, Co Antrim
8 Only 2%
9 No CO_2 emissions so less global warming; no SO_2 emissions so less acid rain; better for wildlife than allowing climate change to go on
10 Noise pollution or visual pollution

TASK 5.2 (page 66)

Three of: Madrid, Barcelona, Bilbao, Alicante   One: Meseta
Two: climate, relief

TASK 5.3 (page 69)

1	F	2	T	3	T	4	F	5	T	6	F	7	T	8	T	9	F

TASK 5.4 (page 70)

Affects	Increase	How	Decrease	How
Birth rate	Children needed to work	People need children for the money they can earn, so they have more	Reliable contraception	Helps people decide how many children they want
			People getting married later	People have less time to have babies
Death rate	Lots of elderly people	More of every 1000 are elderly so are more likely to die.	Clean water	Stops people catching diseases from dirty water
			Sewage system	Stops people catching diseases from sewage
			Good hospitals	Medical treatment available so people are less likely to die of many illnesses
			Good food	People are better nourished and more likely to survive illness
			Vaccinations	Prevent certain fatal diseases

TASK 5.5 (page 71)

1 e   2 b   3 a   4 d   5 h   6 c   7 f   8 g

TASK 5.6 (page 72)

1 c   2 a   3 b

TASK 5.7 (page 73)

1 a   2 b   3 c

TASK 5.8 (page 73)

Socio-economic impacts of aged dependency in MEDCs

	Costs	Benefits
Social	• Adults giving up careers to care for elderly relatives • Strain on carers	• Elderly can provide wise advice • Relatives may be able to provide childcare
Economic	• Expensive health care for the elderly • Meals on wheels and home helps • Pensions • Residential homes needed	

Socio-economic impacts of youth dependency in LEDCs

	Costs	Benefits
Social	• Lack of school buildings and facilities • Lack of teachers • Lots of young adults entering the labour market • Strain on primary schools – some operate 2 half-day sessions for different groups of pupils	
Economic	• Large numbers of infant vaccinations needed	• Lots of young adults entering the labour market – can be good for industry

TASK 5.9 (page 76)

The country they leave: –, +, +   The migrants: +, –, –, +, +
The country people go to: –, +, +, +, –

TASK 5.10 (page 77)

a Opportunity – variety of cultures, broadening experience
b Opportunity – different types of food available
c Challenge – racial tension, misunderstanding, fear
d Challenge – people of other backgrounds may feel excluded, afraid. Opportunity – people can access services they need or may find new foods to try etc

e Opportunity – variety of experiences. Challenge – some people may see it as a threat to the local culture
f Opportunity – variety of experiences, pupils have the chance to learn a language which may get them a job later on, and may help communities understand each other better
g Challenge – some elderly people may find this intimidating.

TASK 5.11 (page 78)

Fig 5.9a – Overpopulation
Fig 5.9b – Underpopulation

TASK 5.13 (page 81)

1 (a) Solar energy, (b) HEP, (c) Wind energy, (d) Geothermal energy, (e) Tidal energy

2 Wave energy

Chapter 6

KNOWLEDGE TEST I

1 See Glossary
2 On York Street, 1 km north of Belfast's CBD, at junction of Westlink, M2 and M3
3 Gallaher's tobacco factory
4 Yorkgate retail and leisure complex
5 350 tertiary jobs
6 See Glossary
7 Motorways and airports
8 Highly qualified and skilled workers including graduates
9 Silicon Glen (the Central Lowlands of Scotland), Silicon Fen (the area around Cambridge), Silicon Strip (the M4 Corridor)
10 Antrim, Galway or Limerick

KNOWLEDGE TEST II

1 Transnational corporation (TNC)
2 Cheaper labour costs (lower average wages of workers)
3 Health and safety regulations **or** regulations to protect the environment
4 MEDC
5 Headquarters in a MEDC
6 One of more and better paid jobs; new skills; increased investment; improved infrastructure
7 Pollution may occur, e.g. air pollution or dumping of waste products
8 One of USA, Japan, UK, Republic of Ireland
9 One of Bangladesh, China, Hong Kong, Indonesia, Malaysia, Philippines, South Korea, Taiwan, Thailand, Vietnam
10 (a) 20,000, (b) 500,000

KNOWLEDGE TEST III

1 (a) Social, (b) Social, (c) Economic
2 LEDCs
3 See Glossary
4 See Glossary
5 Two of increase in number of fish caught; increase in income; jobs created in boat building
6 Kattumarams
7 Spending more on imports than is earned from exports
8 Trade deficit leads to loans and debts which need to be repaid, leaving little money to invest in development
9 Improved health care, education, transport and/or better standard of living
10 Voluntary and short-term

TASK 6.1 (page 84)

Primary: trawler fisherman, coal miner
Secondary: shipyard worker, dressmaker, glass blower
Tertiary: hotel manager, civil servant, insurance salesman, travel agent

TASK 6.3 (page 88)

Transport infrastructure: 3, 5
University links: 2
Quality of environment: 1, 4

TASK 6.5 (page 90)

1 (a) HQ in MEDC
  (b) both MEDCs and LEDCs
  (c) only LEDCs

TASK 6.7 (page 93)

1 economic
2 social
3 social
4 social
5 social
6 economic

TASK 6.8 (page 94)

1 a   2 a   3 a   4 a   5 b   6 b

TASK 6.9 (page 95)

Positive	Negative
Fishermen could continue to catch fish and increase their income	Some materials needed which are not local, e.g. fibreglass
Jobs created in boat building	Use of engines contributes to global warming
Can bring more fish to the shore than they could in the old boats	Uses petrol – a scarce resource. This is not sustainable forever

TASK 6.10 (page 96)

1 Export
2 Import
3 Trade deficit

4 Trade surplus
5 Interdependence

TASK 6.11 (page 97)

LEDCs: raw materials, little, a few, poorer, deficit, harder

MEDCs: manufactured goods, lots of, more expensive

TASK 6.13 (page 100)

1 Voluntary, short-term
2 Bilateral

3 Multilateral, long-term, tied
4 Voluntary, long-term

TASK 6.14 (page 100)

Positive	Negative
Fewer people die of diseases which can be prevented	Aid may be unsuitable
Medical care is provided	Countries get loans and end up in debt, using all their money to pay the interest
People can get an education and better jobs	Doesn't always reach people in most need
People can provide for their families	Governments may be corrupt and spend the money on defence or on luxuries for themselves
People's lives are made easier	Local producers may lose out if there is free food being given out
Saves lives in emergencies	People can become dependent on aid

Chapter 7

KNOWLEDGE TEST I

1 Site
2 A hill top or within a meander bend of a river
3 Roads converge at a bridging point so it is ideal for a market function and therefore likely to grow
4 See Glossary
5 City

6 True
7 False
8 Range
9 Primary school, small grocery shop or newsagent
10 Port, seaside resort

KNOWLEDGE TEST II

1 Push
2 True
3 False
4 Counterurbanisation
5 Green Belt
6 Edge of the city
7 High-rise blocks of flats, e.g. Divis flats
8 Old terraces were run down, overcrowded and lacking electricity, water and heating
9 Loss of inner city jobs; land and buildings left derelict in inner city
10 Fewer local shops left to serve elderly and those without cars; increasing pollution from car use; increased convenience for people living in suburbs

KNOWLEDGE TEST III

1 One of parks created around the Gasworks site; River Lagan cleaned up; 6000 m^2 of public open space provided
2 Two of Waterfront concert hall; W5; Lagan Lookout; public walkways and cycle paths
3 Gregg's Quay **or** Ravenhill Reach
4 8000 jobs
5 Wake up to Waste Campaign; kerbside collection of recyclable waste; increased taxes on waste going to landfill
6 Population growth
7 One of 200 miles of cycle paths; cycle repair facilities; showers at railway station
8 Improved public transport (quality and frequency); cheap fares; integration of bus and rail services
9 No free car parking
10 4000 fewer cars per day

TASK 7.1 (page 103)

a 0–30 metres
b East-facing
c Sheltered from W and SW winds by hills such as Binnagee (2616)
d Carnlough River and other small streams
e Harbour found at grid reference 288181

TASK 7.2 (page 104)

Town, 7, Sharperton and Harbottle, 4.5, 17, Holystone, 2.2, farmsteads, 0.8

TASK 7.3 (page 107)

a Push
b Pull
c Push
d Pull
e Pull

TASK 7.4 (pages 108–109)

1 70
2 75
3 27
4 40
5 LEDCs

TASK 7.5 (page 110)

a MEDC
b LEDC
c Both
d LEDC
e MEDC
f LEDC

TASK 7.7 (page 114)

a Built environment
b Amenities
c Housing
d Waste management
e Employment
f Green spaces

TASK 7.8 (page 114)

a Negative
b Positive
c Positive
d Negative
e Positive
f Negative

TASK 7.9 (page 115)

Reduce, reuse, recycle, compost, incineration, landfill

GLOSSARY TERMS

Afforestation Planting trees.

Aid Resources given by one country or organisation to another country.

Air mass A large body of air with similar temperature and moisture characteristics throughout.

Altitude Height above sea level.

Anticyclone An area of high pressure.

Appropriate technology Technology which uses the skills, and suits the needs and level of wealth of local people.

Atmosphere The layer of air that surrounds the earth.

Biodiversity The number and range of plants and animals in an ecosystem.

Biological weathering Rocks broken down by plants and/or animals.

Biomass The total amount of living matter (plants and animals) within an area or ecosystem.

Biome A very large-scale ecosystem, covering a huge area, with similar soils, plants and animals.

Birth rate The number of live births per 1000 people per year.

Bridging point site A site where a river could be crossed most easily.

Chemical weathering Rocks broken down by chemicals changing the rock or dissolving it away.

Climate The average conditions of the weather taken over a long period of time.

Conservation Protection of resources and landscapes for future generations.

Consumer Animal that gets food by eating something else.

Continentality Distance from the sea.

Convection currents Movements in the semi-liquid mantle which move the plates of the crust.

Counterurbanisation People moving out of cities and towns to rural areas.

Death rate The number of deaths per 1000 people per year.

Decomposers Organisms such as bacteria, which break down dead matter.

Defensive site A settlement site that is easily defended, possibly on a hill-top or inside a meander bend.

Deforestation Cutting down trees.

Deposition Dropping the river's load of eroded material.

Depression An area of low pressure.

Discharge The amount of water passing a point in a certain time.

Distribution of settlements How they are spread out.

Drainage basin The area of land drained by a river and its tributaries.

Earthquake A shock, or series of shocks caused by a sudden earth movement.

Ecosystem A community of plants and animals and the environment they live in, including soil, rock, climate, air and water.

Ecotourism A sustainable form of tourism aimed at protecting ecosystems for visitors to enjoy and also benefiting local communities.

Elements of weather Pressure, precipitation, temperature, wind speed and wind direction.

Emigration When people move out of a country. People who do this are called emigrants.

Erosion Breaking up and removing land.

Ethnic areas Parts of a city where members of specific ethnic groups tend to live close together.

Export When a country sells something abroad.

Fairtrade People who make or grow something are paid a guaranteed fair price for their work.

Flooding When the water in a river is higher than the river bank, so that it overflows.

Fluvial processes Processes operating in rivers (including erosion, deposition, transportation).

Front The boundary between two air masses, separating warm and cold air.

Function The main economic activity of a settlement e.g. port, market town, mining town, and tourist resort.

Functional zones (or land use zones) Areas that have mainly one land use.

Gentrification Inner city areas becoming high-income areas.

Global warming The increased heating of the atmosphere caused by human activities.

Globalisation The way people, goods, money and ideas move round the world faster and more cheaply than ever before.

Hydrological cycle Water cycle in which water is constantly recycled between the sea, air and land.

Igneous rock Rock formed when molten lava or magma cools and hardens.

Immigration When people move into a country. People who do this are called immigrants.

Import When a country buys something from another country.

Industrial location factors The reasons for industry locating in a particular place.

Infrastructure The basic network of transport, water and electricity services that people rely on.

Interdependence The way countries rely on each other for goods and money.

Investment Money coming into a region (or business) in order to create employment, raise the level of economic development (or make a profit).

Irrigation Using water from a river to water the crops.

Latitude Distance from the equator.

Leaching Process where nutrients in the soil are washed away by heavy rainfall.

LEDCs Less economically developed countries, or poorer countries like India or Kenya.

Location Where a settlement is in relation to its surroundings.

Management Decision-making about how an area should be used and protected.

Mechanical weathering Rocks broken down as a result of changes in temperature.

MEDCs More economically developed countries, or richer countries like the UK or the USA.

Metamorphic rock Rock made when other rocks have been altered by extreme heat or pressure.

Migration When people move house permanently.

Millionaire cities Cities with more than 1 million people living in them.

Multicultural society A society containing people from different cultures, races, religions, languages, or nationalities.

Overpopulation Too many people for the resources to support at an adequate standard of living.

Planning A process where decisions are made about how land should be used, what transport and other facilities are needed, and what should be protected.

Plate A segment of the earth's crust that floats on the semi-liquid mantle.

Population change Total population increase or decrease.

Population composition (structure) The way the population is divided between male and female, and different age groups.

Population density The number of people living in a given area, usually 1 km^2.

Population distribution The way in which people are spread out across the earth's surface.

Prevailing winds Most frequently occurring winds blowing towards a place.

Primary industry Obtaining raw materials by extracting them from the earth or sea e.g. farming, fishing, forestry, quarrying and mining.

Producer Green plant that makes its own food from sunlight.

Range The maximum distance that people travel to obtain a service.

Regeneration Taking action to try to give an area new life – improving the buildings, bringing in new employment and providing social facilities.

Relief rainfall Rainfall caused when moist air is forced to rise over mountains.

Resource Something which people can use such as water, farmland, fuel supply, housing.

Resource depletion People using up resources.

Secondary industry Manufacturing a product from either raw materials or components, e.g. furniture-making and car assembly).

Sedimentary rock Rock made from layers of small particles squeezed to form rock.

Settlement A place where people live.

Settlement hierarchy An arrangement of settlements in order of their size and importance.

Site The actual spot where a settlement is built.

Socio-economic area Part of a city where people have similar lifestyles and levels of wealth.

Soil The living and non-living material in which plants grow.

Soil erosion Soil removed by water or wind, or by animals or people.

Sphere of influence The market area of a settlement, i.e. the area from which people travel to use its services.

Sustainability The ability to maintain an environment/ ecosystem so that it survives for future generations.

Sustainable development Improving people's income and standard of living without using up resources, creating pollution or harming people's quality of life.

Sustainable development of cities Cities should grow in a way that meets our needs today without making it difficult for future generations to meet their own needs.

Synoptic charts Weather maps that summarise the weather at a particular time.

Technology The methods or tools which are developed to carry out a task.

Tertiary industry Providing a service to people or businesses, e.g. health, advertising, transport and retailing.

Threshold The minimum number of people needed to ensure that a service will be able to stay in business.

Trade Buying and selling goods and services between one country and another.

Trade deficit When countries spend more money on imports than they earn from exports.

Transportation Carrying along eroded material (load).

Underpopulation Not enough people to use the resources effectively.

Urban fringe The egde of the city.

Urbanisation Increasing percentage of people living in towns and cities.

Volcano A mountain, usually cone-shaped, through which lava, ash and gases may erupt.

Waste management How litter and other waste is dealt with.

Weather The day to day condition of the atmosphere.

Weather forecast A prediction of the weather expected in an area.

Weather recording Making daily records of data from weather instruments such as thermometer, barometer and wind vane.

Weathering Breakdown of rocks into small pieces by the weather, without the movement of the rock itself.

Wet point site A site that has water supply as its most important factor.